D0498641

The Biblical Interpreter

The Biblical Interpreter

*An Agrarian Bible in an
Industrial Age*

RICHARD L. ROHRBAUGH

Property of
CBPac
Please return to
Graduate Theological
Union Library

HOLBROOK LIB
PACIFIC SCHOOL
OF RELIGION

FORTRESS PRESS   PHILADELPHIA

CBPac   1978

BS
476
R64

118923

G
Bg

Biblical quotations from the Revised Standard Version of the Bible, copyright 1946, 1952, © 1971, 1973 by the Division of Christian Education of the National Council of the Churches of Christ in the U.S.A., are used by permission.

COPYRIGHT © 1978 BY FORTRESS PRESS

All rights reserved. No part of this publication may be reproduced, stored in a retrieval system, or transmitted in any form or by any means, electronic, mechanical, photocopying, recording, or otherwise, without the prior permission of the publisher.

Library of Congress Cataloging in Publication Data

Rohrbaugh, Richard L   1936-
    The Biblical interpreter.

    Includes bibliographical references.
    1. Bible—Hermeneutics.   2. Preaching.
I. Title.
BS476.R64   220.6′3   78-54560
ISBN 0-8006-1346-5

7114C78   Printed in the United States of America   1-1346

Contents

Preface

The present work had its beginnings in the actual processes of parish hermeneutics. A ministry that attempts to take the biblical literature as a serious partner in the ongoing dialogue of God's people almost inevitably raises questions about the integrity of what is being done. In sermons, adult classes, or any other context in which the Bible is used in the life of the parish, methods of interpretation are employed that are rarely, if ever, examined with a critical eye. Habits of interpretation easily develop that determine the outcome of biblical usage but that may consist of little more than the consultation of a few familiar commentaries as a preface to reading Scripture in ways that seem "natural" in the context of a given parish or community. As recent developments in hermeneutical theory make clearer the necessity for examining the *entire* process by which the text becomes a sermon, these interpretative habits and methods of the parish preacher become increasingly open to critical analysis and reflection.

Hermeneutics is essentially a task of translation—not in the narrow sense of reduplicating the words of one language into the more or less equivalent words of another, but rather in the broader sense of re-creating meaning in new and different contexts. How one goes about doing that, including the methods used, depends on the list of factors in the situation one conceives as potentially blocking the translation. In the past these factors were considered largely theological, but in more recent

7

times the list of such items has grown. Liberal theology of the nineteenth century conceived the issues in historical terms, and hence sought a historical foundation for the task of translation. Following Bultmann, others have conceived of the issues in existentialist terms, and thus sought existentialist tools as an aid to interpretation. Most recently, linguistic philosophy has raised the issues from yet another point of view by asking how language functions in the human community and whether it does or does not create (re-create?) events of human meaning. What has become obvious in recent years is that the hermeneutical task is in reality a much broader and more complex one than that of merely deducing a few rules by which to read the Bible.

As soon as these wider dimensions of the hermeneutical task come into view, it becomes obvious that it is just as important to take into account the interpreter as it is the literature he is interpreting. Put another way, the sociology, and most particularly the sociology of the knowledge, of the interpreter becomes yet another ingredient in the total task of translating the message for our day.

Because this is so, it is the pastor, as the one who most regularly and most often interprets Scripture in the life of the church, who becomes a link in the hermeneutical chain that stretches from the biblical literature itself, through the varied scholarly processes that raise the questions cited above, and finally to the particular person who is doing the interpreting in the church. To somehow assume that either the theologian, the existentialist philosopher, the historian, or the linguistic analyst can, by running the Scriptures through the insights of their respective disciplines, finally produce a message that will be meaningful in the churches is to lose sight of the fact that it is finally a particular pastor in a particular congregation who is doing the preaching. We cannot presume that hiding out somewhere is a "correct" interpretation of Scripture which, when finally uncovered for us by scholars, can then simply be repeated on Sunday morning by the preacher. The context and person of the one doing the interpreting is a key link in the process of re-creating the meaning of the Scriptures in the church.

The work that follows is thus an attempt to look at one aspect of the total task of translation: the sociological conditioning of both the text and its modern interpreter, which creates potential roadblocks in the translation process. It is done out of the conviction that a critical examination of the *interpreter's* context is a key part of the hermeneutical task, and one that has heretofore received insufficient attention on the part of preachers who are actually doing the interpreting in the church. Even at the level of academic scholarship the issue has been only partially addressed. We are by now used to hearing questions raised about the historical context of the text or, as Bultmann has done, about the existential context of text and interpreter, but rarely have sociological questions been raised about either the text or the interpreter. Nor have we often examined the sociology of our knowledge as we go about the interpretative task. It therefore seems appropriate that persons involved in the actual task of interpretation in the parish should begin to look critically at their own part in the total hermeneutical process.

To do so from the perspective of sociology and the sociology of knowledge is obviously no more inclusive a direction from which to come at the hermeneutical task than was Bultmann's existentialistic analysis. Each has a contribution to make that must then be kept in perspective. An exhaustive analysis of the contextual peculiarities of both text and interpreter could include the raising of questions from many points of view. Psychological, political, and even aesthetic questions can be asked, as well as historical or sociological ones. The present inquiry is therefore offered as a significant but limited contribution to the examination of the total process. It has been chosen for study because it so directly affects what is done as the Scripture is used in the day-to-day life of the Christian community.

A troublesome problem throughout the writing of this work has been the need to find a more inclusive style of language.

Masculine pronouns which infer that biblical interpretation or preaching is always done by males is neither accurate for the present situation nor expressive of an inclusive theology. Attempts to find a more inclusive terminology are rightly going on in our society today, but as yet no genuinely happy solution has appeared. Attempts to use terms like "himself/herself" were made in an original draft of the manuscript but in many instances resulted in sentences that were simply too complex and awkward to follow. In some instances sentences were recast to substitute inclusive plurals rather than masculine-singular forms. Doing this to the entire manuscript, however, would frequently substitute an awkward inclusiveness for simplicity and clarity.

As a very poor compromise, therefore, we have chosen to express our concern at the outset that the reader not allow the inadequacy of our language to imply that biblical study is a masculine pursuit. The outstanding contributions currently being made by female biblical scholars deserve more recognition than our language is presently able to convey.

A case in point is the contribution to the following study made by Dr. Anne Wire. Both her editorial assistance and her constant insistence on the use of the biblical text rather than mere theorizing about it have been of immense value. Her sense of integrity in the use of the biblical materials has been both refreshing and helpful throughout. I also wish to thank Dr. Herman Waetjen and especially Dr. Marvin Chaney of San Francisco Theological Seminary for their encouragement and insights in the pursuit of this project. Their own research into the sociological context of the biblical text has been a major impetus in my effort to pursue the sociological questions in relation to contemporary preaching.

Lastly, I wish to thank both Patty Holt and Louise Evans for their care in the typing of the manuscript and the checking of references. Their effort to carry out this work with dispatch and accuracy is much appreciated.

1

Introduction

To a degree our present confusion in the church about how to bring the New Testament message to contemporary expression is a function of the complexity and confusion of modern life. Along with our growing awareness of the multidimensional character of the human enterprise has come a seemingly endless number of subcategories among the scholarly disciplines attempting to articulate what is going on. This process of increasing specialization has meant that New Testament theology, like any other articulation of human experience, must run the gauntlet of a whole variety of sophisticated scholarly disciplines before it can claim normative significance. It is no wonder that so many would-be interpreters of the biblical message approach the task of preaching with a certain hesitation and bewilderment.

James M. Robinson has expressed the concern this way:

> The task of New Testament theology is to hear the [biblical] texts in such a way as to bring to expression their valid content so that it emerges as a serious alternative for modern times, capable of being decided for or against, without being falsified in this process of translation into modern alternatives.[1]

That is exactly the task of the preacher. Yet it is no longer possible to view hermeneutics as a simple matter of reduplicating the words of Scripture in a modern idiom. What was once a fairly manageable set of rules for interpretation has now become a whole series of disciplines through which the text must be passed. Literary and historical criticism, philology, existentialistic analysis, and of late, linguistic analysis—all have contributions to make and questions to raise. The growing awareness in recent years of the historically conditioned nature of all literary texts, together with the increasing perception that many of our presumably historical statements in the past were in fact theological presuppositions brought to the text ahead of time, has made the use of sophisticated hermeneutical tools necessary. But the resulting complexity and confusion has led beleaguered preachers to rely increasingly on the scholarly world to produce definitive interpretations of a text on their behalf or, on the other hand, to abandon the complexities of hermeneutics altogether and simply preach what they have been handed by their particular tradition.

As if these complexities of the interpretive task were not enough to confound us, our difficulties are multiplied because biblical interpretation represents in acute form the dilemma of contemporary theology over whether God-language is possible at all. It is, after all, not a very long step from questioning the ability of contemporary language to make assertions about God to abandoning altogether the attempt to understand theological language that is two thousand years old. In a sense two gaps stand between the interpreter and the text: the gap of *understanding* that exists between the ancient author and the modern interpreter, and the *existential* gap between the interpreter and *any* theological assertion that claims normative significance. The first gulf to be bridged—that of understanding—is to a large degree a historical one, and in addressing it the hermeneutical task is to find means of allowing the text to speak again what it once said. But the other gap—the existential one—raises the question of whether the ancient text, once we have understood it, says anything that is in a real sense *theological* and thus able to claim the attention of anyone but the historian. That is, can the message be interpreted in such a way that we today have reason to bother with it at all? Can some experiential consanguinity between text-writer and interpreter be found that allows the interpreter to see in the text the same kind of serious existential significance as the writer did? In the fullest sense, then, the hermeneutical task involves both the attempt to understand what the text once said and the articulation of that content in such a way that its message becomes a serious alternative for us today.

Another way of stating the problem is to acknowledge Schleiermacher's pioneering view that a theory of interpretation must encompass *all* the conditions under which understanding of the text becomes possible. While Schleiermacher's own view of what is involved may now be obsolete, his basic insight is still valid and has indeed become the basis of modern hermeneutical theory. As Gerhard Ebeling has pointed out, *"The primary phenomenon in the realm of language is not understanding of language, but understanding through language."*[2] That is, the gap between ourselves and the biblical text cannot be closed by means of historical criticism alone, as if the only hindrance to understanding were that of regaining the historical referents of the words used. We also must ask what the text points to in the way of human event that it intends should come into being for the reader. Having learned this, we must then inquire about the conditions under which that same event can occur today. This inevitably involves us as much in the situation of the interpreter (a point to which we must return later) as it does that of the text being interpreted. It means that unless biblical study is to be merely a game for antiquarians, we must ask about the meaning of the text in light of the philosophical and existential conditions under which language creates and interprets experience.[3]

From the preacher's point of view, we are acknowledging the need to inquire about the conditions under which the text becomes a sermon. As Ebeling has put it, *"The sermon is the* execution *of the text.* It carries into execution the aim of the text. It is proclamation of what the text has proclaimed."[4] The point is that the text, understood by means of exposition and historical inquiry, now itself becomes a hermeneutical aid in the interpretation of *present* experience. Or, to describe it as Bultmann has done, analysis of the text (either historical or existential) has as its purpose speaking to us decisively (*existentiell* in German), that is, in such a way as to involve us in the choices and decisions of life in the present.[5]

What the approach of Bultmann, Ebeling, and their followers requires is the placing of the business of interpretation into both the public and the special theological arena at the same time. The tools of historical criticism are available in a public way for use on literary texts of any kind, including the Bible. Bultmann and others have specifically acknowledged that this is necessary in order that the biblical literature speak in the public arena.[6] But historical criticism alone, by virtue of its proper independent, critical stance, does not admit us into the theological circle. It does not give us the basis for saying anything more than what the text once meant to say.[7] If we are to claim that the text is an aid to interpreting the *present* human situation, and, indeed, to confronting us with choices and decisions, then it is necessary to inquire about the *present* conditions under which the text can fulfill that role. This latter inquiry, which takes us deeply into the situation of the interpreter, is what has led Ebeling, Fuchs, and others to see that if the hermeneutical process is nothing more than exegesis—the interpretation of the text—we are at a dead end. Hence their insight that it is ultimately not the text (we might say, not the text alone) that is interpreted, but the interpreter himself![8] Robert Funk has argued that the whole flow of traditional biblical criticism must change. Instead of the interpreter attempting to lay hold of the text, hermeneutics must become the effort "to allow God to address man through the medium of the text."[9]

What this finally comes down to is the need to take seriously the position of the one doing the interpreting. And since this in the final analysis is most often the preacher in the local parish, the role of the preacher in the whole hermeneutical chain that stretches from the text, through the various critical disciplines, to the persons affected by the text becomes of critical importance. An examination of the conditions under which the actual preaching is done is an important part of the hermeneutic of which Funk speaks, and it is the spelling out of at least some of these conditions of actual preaching that will be our primary concern in what follows.

Before we attempt to indicate exactly where this inquiry will center, it is important to specify the reasons for the direction chosen. We cannot, after all, presume to elucidate *all* possible hindrances that stand between the text and its hearers, hence the need to identify the limits of the study.

We have already alluded to the need for finding some experiential consanguinity between the author of the ancient text and the contemporary interpreter. Without this kind of link our interpretation would remain a purely historical exercise. Moreover, it is precisely this kind of link that allows us to argue that the text has *theological*, that is, normative, significance for us today. Without such links the word that the text presumes to interpret can make no claim upon us.

For Rudolf Bultmann, upon whose work much contemporary New Testament theology rests, the consanguinity of experience between author and interpreter lies in their common existential concern. Both the author and the interpreter presuppose a common experience of the structure of human existence and its possibilities. This common experience shapes the questions which the interpreter brings to the text and to which the text responds.[10] The text, the author, the interpreter, and indeed the human race in general share a common existential concern for the meaning of life. This is what gives us a basis for the claim that the text can address its hearers now in the same fashion that it did originally.

As well taken as Bultmann's point is, however, it does not go far enough and has rightly been criticized as too narrow a basis on which to justify preaching. The question is simply: Is existential concern the *only* link between ourselves and the biblical authors? Or, perhaps, has Bultmann elucidated *all* that is properly included under the rubric of existential concern? That is, what is the scope of the conditions under which the author and the contemporary hearer can be said to share a common ground?

As soon as the question is put this way it becomes obvious that there is more to say than Bultmann has said. Dorothee Soelle, in commenting upon Bultmann's sense of the gospel's liberating power, has asked

> if this openness to which the Gospel frees us can be conceived unpolitically, by ignoring life's decisive possibilities and fates? In the theoretical point of departure for existentialism, as Bultmann understands it, there is no basis for the fact that Bultmann *de facto* limits men's openness to individual existence. [Italics mine.][11]

The criticism is significant because it points to the limiting scope of Western individualism that still pervades theology and, in so doing, raises the question of whether the links between ourselves as hearers of the word and the ancient authors of the text are not more than purely individual. The existential situation that we share in common with persons in the biblical period may include social and political features that Bultmann's individualistic analysis did not take into account. By giving attention to this *corporate* aspect of the human enterprise, which is admittedly a supplement to Bultmann's approach and not to be seen in place of it, we can broaden the base on which the claim to consanguinity of experience can be made. On the other hand, should our inquiry indicate points of disjunction in human experience between our own day and that of the biblical writers, we will have a basis for making the necessary transpositions that will make the text's intention clear (or for limiting our claims about what the text is able to say should transposition prove impossible).

Our intent in what follows, then, will be to focus on the sociological situation of the interpreter. We do so with the understanding that both historical criticism and individualistic existential analysis are appropriately part of the whole hermeneutical task. The case for those items has been made so often and so well, however, that most preachers today understand the need for them. The justification for asking *sociological* questions about the relation between the author and the interpreter has not been made, and that is the primary intent of the present inquiry.

Our general thesis can be summarized this way: the biblical literature of both Old and New Testaments was written in and to agrarian societies and preindustrial cities but is being interpreted today (at least in most American churches) in industrial societies in which the social perception of reality is markedly different from that of the biblical period. Moreover, if it is true as stated above that (because he is the one who most regularly interprets the Scripture in the church) the preacher is a key link in the hermeneutical chain, then it can be argued that without this focus on the potential for social consanguinity between the biblical writers and the modern preacher the entire hermeneutical process is aborted immediately prior to its fruition in the life of the Christian community. Our justification for asking about the sociology of the preacher's setting is thus seen to rest on a hermeneutical understanding in which preaching itself needs justification as a process of allowing the text to be heard theologically as well as historically.

In the hope of reaching worthwhile conclusions about the preacher's task in light of the above, it is our intent to move through the following process. We shall begin our inquiry into the sociological context of both the interpreter and the author by a brief study of macrosociology aimed at highlighting sociological concerns relevant to interpretation. We need to look at the agrarian society and the preindustrial city and compare them to our own industrial society in such a way as to dramatize the uniqueness of each as the respective contexts for author and interpreter. If those respective contexts can be brought to consciousness, we will then have the basis for asking the deeper and more important questions about the sociology of the interpreter's knowledge. That is, we will have a basis for asking about the sociological conditioning of the preacher's perception of the world, together with how that might or might not affect what he understands the biblical text to mean. We will focus on the fact that the Scriptures were written by and for persons whose perceptions of reality were conditioned by an agrarian and preindustrial society, while it is being interpreted by and for hearers in an industrial world. Our objective will be not only to uncover a potential roadblock to understanding but also to suggest some of the transpositions necessary if consanguinity between ourselves and the biblical writers is to be maintained.

At this point an obvious problem arises. Since the sociology of the knowledge of each individual interpreter is different, a full accounting of the implications of what we are doing would require a limitless number of profiles of particular preachers working in particular situations. This is clearly not possible. So in order to put all we have been talking about to the test of actual interpretation, we will examine the work of well-known contemporary preachers and ask what might have been the particular sociology of their knowledge that led them to interpret as they did. We shall also ask how their expositions of particular texts might stand the scrutiny of comparison with the way those same texts would have been viewed in the sociological context of agrarian societies or preindustrial cities. To do this, we must become involved with interpreting the text ourselves. While this exercise will not give us the basis for generalizing to conclusions that are valid for all preachers everywhere (since each obviously lives in a unique situation), we should be able to highlight the kinds of questions the preacher ought to ask himself as he interprets both the text and himself.

Finally, we must draw what conclusions we are able, both for the preacher who is attempting to interpret biblical texts and for the larger hermeneutical task itself. We will attempt to show that as valuable as the various contributions to the job of translation made by the multiplying disciplines have been, the task of interpretation is essentially incomplete until we conceive of hermeneutics as including the particularity of the person(s) doing the interpreting. Put another way, until the preacher understands the role he and his society play in executing the intention of the text, the job is incomplete. It is simply not enough to take the results of the critical disciplines and repeat them on a Sunday morning as a supposedly objective interpretation of the text's intended word.

2

The Social and Historical Dimensions of Preunderstanding

The interpretation of any ancient literary text would be impossible if its expressions of life were completely strange to the modern reader. Not only is *some* ground of common experience essential for understanding, but it also makes the effort to understand worthwhile. Biblical interpretation thus presupposes a persistence through the centuries of the essentials of human experience, what we have called a consanguinity of experience between author and modern interpreter.[1]

According to Wilhelm Dilthey, the basis of our ability to understand literary texts (or even ordinary conversation with others) is our own experience. By reflecting on the meanings and patterns of our own experience and our own thought, we are able to analogize to new complexes of meaning we are attempting to understand.[2] The process of coming to new understandings is thus heavily dependent upon our ability to relate these new matters to types and categories of knowledge we already possess.

Why this is so is not difficult to grasp. In their book *The Social Construction of Reality*, Peter Berger and Thomas Luckmann draw a distinction that clarifies what is going on as we try to understand new meanings. They describe what they call the "reality of everyday life," that is, that picture of reality we all have which derives from our immediate everyday experience and which forms the frame of reference against which we judge outside suggestions.[3] This reality of everyday life we all take for granted *as* reality. It does not require additional verification beyond its simple presence. It is simply there. I *know* that it is real.[4] Whether it is, of course, is beside the point. It is nevertheless the standard by which I judge all other meanings.

Contrasted with this "reality of everyday life" are what Berger and Luckmann label "provinces of finite meaning."[5] By this they mean those enclaves of meaning that lie essentially outside common-sense reality and that have finite boundaries, limits, and modes of experience.[6] Moving into one of these provinces of finite meaning is like seeing the curtain temporarily lifted on a stage. Attention is shifted away from everyday reality and a certain tension is introduced between it and the finite sphere. "The paramount [everyday] reality envelops [these finite spheres of reality] on all sides, as it were, and consciousness always returns to the paramount reality as from an excursion."[7] Once again, it is irrelevant whether such finite realities *actually* exist; what is important is that we perceive that they exist.

This distinction of Berger and Luckmann is germane to our discussion of biblical interpretation because religion, like art or philosophy, is an endemic producer of "finite provinces of meaning." Religion frequently introduces problematic interruptions—assertions or ideas that don't seem real or verifiable in everyday reality—into our common-sense scheme of things, and thus requires constant rationalization to fit the relatively unproblematic routines of everyday experience.

The basic form in which these perceptions of reality are objectivized is language:

> It is this edifice of semantic fields, categories, and norms which structures the subjective perceptions of reality into a meaningful, cohesive and "objective" universe. This universe, "reality as seen" in a culture, is taken for granted in any particular society or collectivity. For the members of a society or collectivity it constitutes the "natural" way of interpreting, remembering and communicating individual experience.[8]

In a sense this way of seeing and interpreting is internal to the individual, but at the same time it is also external to him as that universe in which he *and* his contemporaries exist and act.[9] That is, the individual's universe of perception is both his own, colored by his own unique personality and experiences, and at the same time that of his society, which is largely responsible for both giving and maintaining all structures of meaning. Such universes of meaning are both precarious (needing constant legitimation in the face of the great crises of life) and reinforced by both language and the institutional structures of a society.

What this means is that the individual views the world with what has been called preunderstanding. He sees the world through a socially derived and socially maintained set of perceptions that he brings to any encounter with new suggestions or new meanings. This realization has led biblical scholars such as Rudolf Bultmann to focus critical attention on the preunderstanding brought to the biblical text ahead of time by anyone wishing to interpret it. One cannot understand a text unless particular questions are asked of it, and these questions are prompted and informed by the preunderstanding of the world the interpreter carries with him as he initially approaches the text.

Here again we confront the issue of finding a rationale for reading and interpreting the biblical text in our own day. For Bultmann, we do so because both we and the biblical authors *share a consanguinity of preunderstanding* that prompts questions of *mutual* concern. The texts can speak to us because we, like they, share a concern for questions about the structure and meaning of human existence to which faith is an answer.[10] Moreover, it is this shared preunderstanding that enables the interpreter to analogize from the proclamation of the author to his own contemporary experience. Without that common bond in at least some degree, the Scriptures would be not only difficult to understand but probably of interest only to the purest of historians.

The one qualification of Bultmann's view of the hermeneutical process we have noted so far is Robinson's complaint that preunderstanding involves more than psychological inwardness and is indeed, as Berger and Luckmann have pointed out, to a significant degree both given and maintained for the individual by his society. An additional qualification that will become of key importance as our study proceeds is suggested by Robert Funk. He argues that Bultmann's method presumes the existence of a *universally* applicable interpretation. He then comments:

> An interpretation that is universally applicable cannot, without further consideration, be brought into relation to the specific existence of a given period or individual. That is to say, the human situation must be *interpreted* in terms of the concrete existence of a particular community or person.[11]

The point is simple but crucial. There is no such thing as an *uninterpreted* point of view from which interpretation can begin. Hence, when one begins to interpret language that has a historical location prior to one's own, the tendency is to see it in terms of *one's own* perception of the preunderstood subject matter rather than that which may be unique to the original writer. Even preunderstanding that is shared by author and interpreter is nonetheless held by each in historically and sociologically conditioned fashion. This problem is magnified, moreover, when dealing with literature from another culture. All the cultural loadings of any shared or preunderstood interest then come into play and must be taken into account. We conclude, therefore, that even though a shared set of preunderstandings is a proper place for biblical interpretation to begin, all preunderstanding, just as all other knowledge, is historically, sociologically, and culturally conditioned.

It is ironic that a positivist historicism was the context out of which an overwhelming sense of the relativity of all human perspectives grew. (The work of Wilhelm Dilthey was done against this background.) From an understanding of the historicity of events, it is not a very long step to seeing the inevitable historicity, and thus inevitable datedness, of human thought about those events. The historicist insistence that no historical situation could be understood except in its own terms can thus be readily translated into an emphasis on the social and historical situation of *thinking* as well as events.[12]

Historical "knowledge" is therefore a function not only of events and the data they produce but also of the historical *Sitz im Leben* of the historian himself. He must write in such a way as to make the object of his historical research understandable to his contemporaries, and is therefore obliged to couch his descriptions in the categories and thought patterns of his own time.

The preacher or biblical interpreter must do the same. Not only must the language into which he translates the biblical text be that of his own time, but also the preunderstanding that he brings to the text in attempting to decipher its meaning will be that of his own day. Funk is correct. Any analysis of the structure of human existence, or the exposition of any other allegedly shared concern between author and interpreter, itself begins from a historically conditioned point of view. The epistemological questions thus raised may call into doubt the very possibility of historical "knowledge" in a theoretical sense, but at a more practical level, and certainly at the level of biblical interpretation, the sociology of our knowledge demands that we at least acknowledge the limitations and distortions that may be introduced into our interpretation by the conditioned nature of the preunderstanding we bring to the text.

By now the complexity of the matter ought to be obvious. The social forces that impinge upon any interpreter and color his thought are far beyond our ability to unravel them. The conditioning of one's national heritage, racial background, socioeconomic status, and even academic heritage—all make the sociology of our knowledge incredibly complex. If one adds to this the personal psychology of the interpreter, highlighted by Dilthey and others, the intricacy of it all boggles the mind.

If, however, the tangle of conditioning that our social perception of reality has created is a bit overwhelming and will probably place limitations on our ability to say definitely what a given text means, the effort to bring to consciousness at least the broad outlines of that conditioning should nonetheless do at least two important things for us in the task of interpretation.

First, by noting some of the similarities and disjunctions in the sociology of the knowledge of both the biblical author and the modern interpreter, we can surmount an additional roadblock to understanding the text correctly. The important qualification on this offered earlier by Robert Funk is the fact that where we discover *disjunctions* between ourselves and the authors we must sharply limit our claims for the universality of our interpretation. What we gain in understanding of the text may thus produce a trade-off: it may become apparent that not all of the text's intention is directly applicable to our own situation—at least not without efforts at transposition. That is a risk that must be taken, however, not only because integrity requires it but also because without it we risk hearing the wrong thing.

A second benefit of raising to consciousness the sociology of the knowledge of the author and interpreter should be an enlargement of the base upon which preaching is justified. That is, it should expand the consanguinity of experience between ourselves and the biblical writers by adding a *social* dimension to Bultmann's already valuable exposition of the common concern for the individual's questions about the meaning of life. By asking what in our *social* perception of reality is similar to that of the biblical writers, we should be able to enrich and deepen our understanding of the common human ground we share with the text, and this, in turn, offers the hope that preaching (or indeed the whole task of interpretation) will be further justified by virtue of a larger reservoir of common concern between the biblical message and our own times. To have discovered *new* common ground gives the partners to *any* dialogue both more reason to talk and greater facility in doing so.

It is perhaps clear, then, why our study can proceed only after we have taken a comparative look at the sociology of the biblical writers and that of our own day. The ethos of the agrarian society and preindustrial city of biblical times is in many ways similar to that of industrial societies, but in many other ways it is quite different. While our survey of these respective societies cannot be exhaustive, enough will have to be said to provide a basis for looking at specific biblical texts in a sociological light. Were such a project undertaken in exhaustive form, its magnitude would be intimidating to both writer and reader, but the case for *beginning* such a program can fortunately be made by looking at these respective societies in outline form—hence it is to that which we now turn. Once that has been accomplished we will have the background from which to ask the needed questions about the sociology of the modern interpreter's perceptions of the text, and then be able to put all we have been discussing into practice in actual interpretation.

3

The Agrarian and Industrial Worlds

Our stated intent is to construct a comparative profile of agrarian and industrial societies in order to give some accounting of the historical and sociological conditioning that colors the preunderstanding of both text and interpreter. In so doing we hope to provide a base for both allowing the text to speak more clearly from its own context, and for us to hear it more clearly from ours.

The title of this chapter needs sharp qualification. No exhaustive sociological profile of the agrarian and industrial societies, in the sense that such might be undertaken by a sociologist of religion, is within our competence. Nor, fortunately, is it necessary. The problem we have set before ourselves can be adequately addressed by giving attention to a summary profile of these two societies that draws upon the expertise of those for whom this is a field of primary research. There is no doubt that were an exhaustive biblical commentary the intent of our labors an equally substantial piece of sociological research would be required, but for our purpose of demonstrating the *initial need for* such a project, a more summary statement will suffice.

A Profile of the Agrarian Society

Agrarian societies began to make their appearance in the fertile valleys of the Middle East some five to six thousand years ago and constituted one of the great social revolutions of antiquity.[1] Their eventual spread both east and west profoundly altered the character of human life and had, as we shall see, significant impact on religious thought as well as on the practical routines of everyday life. The invention of the plow, the discovery of metallurgy, the harnessing of animal power, and the use of the sail and wheel all provided the technology for a revolution in the economic base of the older horticultural societies. In fact it is technological changes such as these, and the ripple effect they have in altering the patterns of life, that most sociologists use as the key variable in distinguishing primitive, agrarian, and industrial societies from each other.[2] As a result of such advancing technology, agricultural surpluses became possible for the first time in sufficient quantity to support substantial numbers of nonagricultural specialists. This in turn provided a major impetus for the rise of the preindustrial city.[3]

Though a great deal of diversity among agrarian societies has led some sociologists to question the typological category, certain common features among them incline many scholars to treat them as a generic type.[4] Among those features of the agrarian world of particular interest to us are the following.

Advances in Technology and Methods of Production[5]

New tools, skills, crafts, the domestication of new animals, new sources of energy, the invention of the iron plow, and countless other small advances in technology such as those just mentioned above all combined to create substantial enlargement of the agricultural surplus. Not only did this make possible the rise of larger urban communities, but it also created trade in the true sense of the word. Both agricultural surpluses and expanded trade were largely the result of the new agriculture that became possible on a mass scale for the first time.

Advances in Military Technology

The development of cavalry and chariot warfare, together with the technologizing of other weaponry, aided in decreasing the significance of the individual as his own weapon-maker and defender. The power of the state increased in direct proportion to the monopoly it held on the means of force. The existence of such standing armies as those maintained by the rulers of these ancient societies also meant, by contrast, the appearance of guerrilla warfare in the modern sense of that term.

Increases in the Size of Territory and Population Controlled by the State

Territories measured in the millions of square miles and populations counted in the millions of persons came into being. This marked the appearance of the first true empires spanning a wide geography and diverse ethnic and cultural groups.[6] It also produced a collectivity of resources hitherto unavailable to those holding political power.

Constant Warfare and Internal Struggle

Most agrarian states came into being through conquest and were maintained by continual warfare with neighboring states.[7] So also internal struggles for power, particularly in societies with ill-defined patterns for political succession, became endemic to the agrarian world.

Monarchical Government

With the exception of a few isolated examples, nearly all agrarian states were ruled by kings or emperors. Military exigencies were such as to create substantial pressures for firm authority and decision-making in times of national emergency. Biblical students are familiar with just this phenomenon in the life of Israel, and doubtless the agonizing over the institution of monarchy recounted in 1 Samuel was not an isolated experience for societies making the transition from the simpler horticultural stage to the more complex agrarian one.

Rise of Urban Communities

Though the urban segment of the population in an agrarian society was never more than a small percentage of the total, urban centers—or preindustrial cities, as Sjoberg has called them—came to dominate the agrarian world politically, culturally, economically, and religiously.[8] From Jericho, perhaps the oldest of such cities, all the way to Rome, the fact of urbanization looms large in the biblical literature.

Vocational Specialization and Developed Trade

Officials, priests, scholars, scribes, merchants, servants, soldiers, craftsmen, laborers, and beggars made up a substantial portion of the urban population. Such diversity and specialization (which is a relative matter since it approached nothing like the specialization of the modern industrial society) meant that workers had to trade the products of their labor for those of others, thus making trade for the first time a significant means of mutual support.[9]

The relation of these preindustrial cities to peasant villages and rural areas was likewise one built on trade, though increasingly this relationship came to be dominated by the cities. The development of writing and coinage, both under the control of the urban privileged classes, soon aided in widening the gulf between peasant and urbanite to the point of open animosity. These cleavages of social class, which characterized virtually all agrarian societies, are one of the most important sociological facts the biblical interpreter must take into account, and therefore a phenomenon to which we must return in some detail later in this study.

Alliance Between Religion and the State

The alliance between religion and the state in the agrarian society calls for slightly more detailed comment. As Gerhard Lenski points out, in most agrarian societies religion was of prime concern to the state, and in most instances this resulted in the state attempting to harness the power of religion in the maintenance and legitimation of the social order.[10] To those familiar with the biblical tradition this is an old story. From "yes-men" prophets around the throne, to the selling of priestly offices, the

phenomenon of the state using religion to legitimate itself is com-
monplace in both Old and New Testaments. Moreover, as Lenski
indicates, in most instances the officialdom of religion was all too
happy to cooperate. Status in society as well as a certain security
that derived from being close to the throne were the obvious
rewards. That too is a familiar story in the Bible.

Two other characteristics of the religious situation in agrarian
societies are of related importance to us. The first is the tendency
for these societies to develop *national* religions. That is, religions
that provided *theological* legitimation of a *particular* state. The
theology of such national faiths is an interesting story in itself,
although we cannot stop to detail it here. We mention this characteristic, however, because important changes in this phenomenon, which will be of interest to us, take place in the industrial
society.

The second related characteristic of the religious situation in
agrarian societies worth noting is the tendency toward increasing
sociological diversity within these states to produce differing versions of the religious heritage and tradition of the group. Something like this undoubtedly lies behind the various pentateuchal
documents commonly differentiated by critical scholars and can
be seen again in the early Christian movement both in the New
Testament period and on into the second century. Such differing
interpretations of the national religious heritage often caused considerable class conflict in the agrarian world, perhaps an early
indicator of the role of the sociology of knowledge in interpreting
religious meaning.[11]

This summary listing of some of the salient features of the
agrarian society provides a background for understanding the
marked social inequalities that were the direct result of agrarian
social institutions. It is common in much of the sociological literature dealing with this period to designate the agrarian society
as a two-class social structure comprised on the one hand of a
small elite class characterized by power, achievements, posses-

sions, education, and certain manners of speech and dress, and on the other by a very large lower class lacking most of these manifestations.[12] In addition to these two large classes, which account for the bulk of the population in and around the cities, there also existed in agrarian societies a group of social outcasts who subsisted on the fringe of every preindustrial city together with the peasant population of the rural areas that constituted the bulk of the total population. In a two-class analysis of the agrarian society these latter groups, the outcasts and the peasants, are usually lumped together with the lower urban classes and treated as a single group.

For many purposes of sociological analysis this rather broad view of a bifurcated social structure is sufficient differentiation for drawing generalizations about the agrarian world. But for our interest in closely identifying the sociological context of biblical passages, the four-class system suggested by Robert Bellah takes fuller account of the situation. Bellah suggests that a significant difference between historic societies (his equivalent of Lenski's agrarian society and Sjoberg's feudal society) and the earlier archaic societies (again, his equivalent of the horticultural society in Lenski's work and the folk society in that of Sjoberg) is the general shift from the simpler two-class social stratification to the more complex four-class system that is characteristic of all the great historic civilizations until early modern times. The four classes Bellah differentiates are: a political-military elite, a cultural-religious elite, an urban lower-class group (merchants and artisans), and the rural lower class (peasants). The only social group not included in this four-class system is the relatively small outcast population on the fringe of the preindustrial city. We make mention of this group here, not only to remind ourselves that the outcasts are a separate group, but also because we shall be dealing with their unique social position in our textual study of Luke 16:19-31 a little later.

Though it is obvious that all Bellah has done is break each of the two-class system's classes down into two additional groups, it is precisely this finer differentiation of the situation that we wish to highlight. As we shall see in a moment, there existed significant differences in the social and religious outlook of these four groups that are of import to the biblical interpreter. Using Robert Bellah's four-class system, then, let us look briefly at the social position and religious perceptions of each group.[13]

The political-military elite formed the core of the power structure in an agrarian society. This group, though never more than 2 percent of the urban population, held virtually total control. It was made up of royal families and high government and military officials. The thinking of these groups was dominated by what Lenski calls "the proprietary theory of the state."[14] In this view the state is "owned" by the one who controls it and is subject to his use for personal gain. This right of ownership extended to the land itself, which in virtually all instances the king claimed not only to own and use for himself but also to pass on to his heirs. This also gave the king the right of taxation. A noble or even a peasant may own the land, but the king owns it too, and may exact his due from it as he chooses. The confiscation of property, the domestic equivalent of foreign conquest, was also widely practiced by agrarian rulers.[15] Though the total number of persons in this political-military elite was never large, there was among them a high degree of cohesion that led to a predictable closing of ranks when threatened from the outside.

The second elite group Bellah differentiates is what he calls the cultural-religious element. Included here would be the priests, scribes, religious and political functionaries, educational specialists, and other literati. Though this group often wielded considerable influence around the seat of power, they are characterized not so much by the control of power as by the role of providing legitimation for it. They are the group who provided both the bureaucratic system for structuring the royal authority into the life of the society and the mythological-theological rationale for the existence and style of the state. Theirs was a stabilizing function upon which depended the maintenance of the social order.

Both of these upper classes were characterized by peculiar

manners of speech, dress, and even personal mannerisms. Class anonymity, to a large degree achievable in the industrial society, was a virtual impossibility in the agrarian world.[16] Among these groups, and indeed among the lower classes of the agrarian world also, marriage was so much the norm that single individuals were a serious cultural anomaly. In contrast to the lower classes, however, elite marriages were parentally arranged with a careful view to the perpetuation of class distinctions. This instinct for self-preservation also gave the upper-class families their characteristic interest in genealogies as a means of ensuring continuity, identity, and cohesion.[17]

Families among the urban elite tended to be large. Contrary to the popular notions of American sociology, the large family was *not* a rural phenomenon in the ancient world.[18] Peasants simply could not afford to support large families on their small plots of land. The extended family, of which the genealogy was a symbol, served some of the same purposes as does the welfare system of an industrial city (care of the aged, recovery of losses from accidents, care of orphans, etc.), and was clearly the luxury of the rich.

Ironically, the position of women in the upper classes of the agrarian world was severely restricted—exactly the reverse of the situation in the industrialized society. Upper-class women had almost no contact with males outside their immediate family and were carefully isolated from contact with the lower classes. This meant that from six or eight years of age until the time of their arranged marriage, they lived in a largely female world.

In Max Weber's classic study of the sociology of religion, careful attention is given to the religious attitudes of the agrarian social classes. It is partly because we find divergence here between the two upper classes of Bellah's four-class system that his more nuanced differentiation is worth making.

The political-military elite are generally characterized by a lack of interest in religion, or, as Weber puts it, "the warrior nobles have not really become the carriers of a rational religious ethic."[19]

That is, they do not require of what religious interest they do have much beyond protection against evil magic or such ceremonial rites as befit their caste. Though they, like all classes in society, could often get caught up in the religious reforms of prophetic movements, their real interest lay not in reform but in prophetic promises of divine aid in the course of war. The prayer for victory was their primary use of religious language.

The other elite group in agrarian societies, the religious-cultural elite, was in a slightly different position. Their religious interest was directed toward the legitimization of the existing order and the ritualistic controls required to maintain that. Seeing the ruler as divine or, if not himself a god, at least the direct representative of the gods provided cosmic justification for the status quo of both the political and religious hierarchies. Most students of the ancient world are familiar with the abundant mythological material that carries this connotation. These religious functionaries and cultural intellectuals tended thus to be extremely conservative and were no more interested in prophetic reforms than their political counterparts. Their interest in religion was to control the system by means of religious conventions. When they, along with other elements of society, got caught up in prophetic reform, they quickly found ways to routinize it, despising as they did all forms of irrational or passionate religious fervor.[20]

The third of Bellah's four groups is what he calls the lower-class urbanites. These are the merchants, artisans, craftsmen, traders, government retainers, and skilled and unskilled laborers who made up the bulk of the city population. Since the pre-industrial city possessed no true middle class in our modern sense, the gulf between these lower-class people and the upper classes was substantial. Their manners, dress, speech, and level of education were all markedly different from those of the upper classes.

Among these people marriage was less likely to be arranged and likely to occur at a very young age. There was a double standard of sexual morality for males and females, and romantic love, such as is known in the industrial society, was rare. Social isolation for women was not, however, as great as that among the upper classes simply because there was no way to arrange it. Women were more likely to work alongside men, and, in fact, the further down the social scale and the nearer to the rural life of the peasant we come, the more likely this was to be true.

Weber indicates that among these lower urban classes great religious diversity existed. In some cultures or cities they evidenced no particular interest in religion, but in many others it was this group that was the strikingly innovative and religiously sensitive one in society. In contrast to the cultic and routinized religion of the upper classes, the lower-class urbanites were, in Weber's terminology, the bearers of rationalized, ethical religion.[21] By that he means a religion that carried forward a rationalized attempt to shape life according to some ethical or moral vision.

A dominant motif of the religion of the lower urban classes was that of "salvation."[22] The upper classes, using religion to legitimate the status quo, talked not of salvation but of protection. The lower classes, however, aspired to what they did not have and therefore articulated that void in soteriological language. While the early religion of artisans and merchants was often totemistic and magical, it frequently broke through to prophetic visions of a new society and the promise of a new order. Weber argues that this was especially true in newly emerging cities.[23] He also sees lower-class religion as having about it a "pariah" quality. By the term "pariah people," Weber means a distinctive, hereditary social group which is politically and socially disprivileged, which lacks political autonomy, which uses taboos to prevent intermarriage and commensality with outsiders, and which above all has a strong hope of salvation for the group.[24] This in turn causes the members to cling to each other and to their status as a disprivileged people whose "day" is promised. Both Judaism and Christianity evidence this pariah mentality, which is to be expected since both movements emerged among the lower classes of the preindustrial city. Both have also retained to a large degree the characteristic soteriological hope of lower-class urban religion.

In this regard it is fascinating to note Weber's documentation of the tendency among lower-class city people to form congregations—worshiping religious communities. Here more than anywhere else one sees the characteristic corporate mind-set of the agrarian world coming into play.

The last of the four classes we are differentiating in the agrarian society is that of the peasants. These people lived primarily in the rural areas, though in some instances peasants were located on the fringe areas of the cities themselves. Though treated in the same fashion as outcasts by the upper classes, the peasantry was really a group distinct from the prostitutes, beggars, and derelicts that inhabited every preindustrial city's outer fringes. By and large the peasants were farmers and thus the largest single group in the population.

They were not, however, the bearers of much influence. By manner, clothing, and speech they were easily identifiable and were separated from the lower urban classes by nearly as large a gulf as that between themselves and the urban elite. Marriage did not take place between peasants and the lower urban class, nor did many of the peasants ever aspire to anything other than that to which they were born.

Ironically it was the peasant women of all the females in an agrarian society who enjoyed the most freedom and respect in the male world. They worked in the fields alongside the men and were an integral part of the rural economic structure. In the rural society, as in much of the rest of society during earlier periods, women were even accorded a modest voice and respect in matters of religion. They occasionally were recognized as having charismatic gifts and at least in several biblical instances were accorded the title "prophet."

Contrary to popular imagination today, neither political nor religious reform has been characteristic of the rural peasant. The pariah complex that dominated the thinking of the lower urban classes was almost wholly absent among the peasants, who tended to be the carriers of religious reform only when they and their society were threatened from the outside.[25]

What religion did exist among the peasants of most agrarian societies tended to be irrational, magical, and directly related to the need to implore the gods for better crops.[26] Because of this, and also because of their isolation from the cultic centers in the cities (which made participation in cultic ritual difficult for them), both the urban rich and the urban poor looked upon the peasants as religiously unclean. The pejorative connotation that came to be placed upon the term *am ha aretz* in Palestine in the time of Jesus is an illustration of the point.[27] These people of the land were considered ignorant of the law, and since they did not observe its prescriptions regularly they were designated as religiously impure. Such attitudes toward the peasantry are well attested in rabbinic literature as well as in the New Testament itself.

An almost humorous example is afforded by the mental gymnastics this required for those of the city who, by virtue of living near the Temple in Jerusalem, practiced the prescribed religious rites with regularity and thus considered themselves levitically pure, yet who distastefully recognized the necessity of doing business with the agricultural areas and the impious peasants. By the time of the second century after Christ an accommodation had been reached through which the country folk who lived within a reasonable distance of the city of Jerusalem were regarded as *generally* observant of the law and therefore declared pure. An imaginary line was drawn around Jerusalem at a distance of about fifteen miles (through the village of Modin) and those within it were declared trustworthy. Those beyond it were suspect. The Mishnah states it baldly:

> On the hither side of Modin the peasants are trusted regarding the purity of their earthenware; beyond it they are not trusted. Thus it happens that when a potter selling his pots passes Modin on the way to Jerusalem, though he and his pots are the same as

before, they are now considered pure; if they return past the line of Modin, he is no longer to be believed in regard to their purity.[28]

Many studies have been done which indicate that when religion does take hold among the disprivileged lower classes it tends to be messianic. The upper classes, resting their case for honor on a sense of their being as such, see as religious values those that contribute to protection and maintenance. The lower classes, however, resting whatever hope for honor they can muster on the concealed promise of a new future, see religious value in a messianic vision that assigns to them a vocation or mission.[29] Messianism is clearly a vision of change that wells up out of the frustrations of life in a world in which radical differences exist between the lot of the rich and that of the poor. Of that the agrarian religions of the past, and indeed much of the biblical literature itself, are clear illustrations.

With this profile of the agrarian society now before us, it is time to turn our attention to the industrial world of our own day. Our treatment of this pole of the relationship we are considering need not be extensive, not only because it is more familiar to us all but also because our purposes will be amply served by a summary profile of the major differences between the agrarian society and our own. It will be enough to show that we live in a very different kind of world.

Profile of the Industrial Society

The modern industrial society, like each of its predecessors, is the result of significant technological change:

> During the last two centuries, the productive systems of many societies have undergone a profound change. In this relatively short space of time, techniques of production and patterns of economic organization have been replaced by new and radically different ones. These developments have laid the foundation for a new and profoundly different kind of society, the modern industrial.[30]

Again using the work of Gerhard Lenski, let us outline the significant changes wrought by industrialization that have produced the society in which we now live.[31]

Economic Changes

The agrarian society depended largely on the muscle power of either men, women, or beasts, along with a few simple devices for mechanical advantage. Modern industrial societies, with their tremendous consumption of fossil or nuclear fuels, have created inanimate energy sources that have effected a revolution in both production and consumption. Economic self-sufficiency has been replaced with widespread marketing and distribution systems that trade the products of the specialized labor of highly skilled workers. For the first time in history the majority of the population no longer derives its living directly from agriculture, and as a result of this, escalating specialization has given us new kinds of vocational freedom unheard of in the agrarian world. This in turn has been a major contributor to the individualistic outlook of modern times. In the agrarian society there was no value placed on doing one's own thing simply because there was not the opportunity.

Demographic Changes

Both specialization and the decrease in farm labor required to produce our food have combined to create massive changes in the distribution of population. Huge cities and tremendously increased total populations have become possible for the first time. Lower infant mortality rates and longer life expectancy have threatened the world with overpopulation and brought on the necessity of population control. Since children become an economic liability in an industrial society, birth rates fall as industrialization increases. Small families, living in huge urban complexes, have become the dominant social pattern of this era.

Yet another demographic change has been in the configuration of the city itself. In the preindustrial city the core area was the focus of political and religious prestige, and hence the domicile of the upper classes. In the industrial city it is the reverse. That is so because the centers of activity and power in an industrialized world can be more diverse and scattered. In the preindustrial city, with neither electronic communication nor automobiles, access to the centers of power required living in the center of the city. It is also worth noting that whereas in the preindustrial city the pace of life was slow and activity virtually confined to the daylight hours, in the industrial world time has become a scarce and marketable commodity requiring that all twenty-four hours of the day be utilized for production.

Political Changes

Monarchy has virtually disappeared in the industrial countries of the world. Its vestigial remains in societies such as Great Britain have little governmental significance. Republican forms of government are not universal in the industrial world, but they predominate and are symbolic of the dramatic change that has occurred in the role government plays. It is no longer the province of a few to be used for self-aggrandizement. Proprietary rights have disappeared. Government is organized to handle thousands of previously unknown tasks in the service of society. The rapid increase of military power among industrialized states, accompanied by a rising nationalism, has created the first truly worldwide empires and equally has brought on their demise as the military power of surrounding nations likewise emerged.

Educational Changes

Education in the industrial state is no longer an adjunct of the religious institutions of society. Nor is it limited to a privileged few. Literacy is virtually universal, and education in general plays a vastly greater role in the shaping and legitimization of the state than in the agrarian world. In this respect education ironically fulfills many of the functions that religion once did in the agrarian world. In his book *Deschooling Society*, Ivan Illich has made just this suggestion.[32] He argues that the priesthood of the modern industrial world is the faculty and administration in the public school system!

A presupposition of this emphasis on education in industrialized societies has been the belief that we are masters of our own future rather than the helpless victims of fate we were construed to be by agrarian cultures. The scientific revolution, together with increasingly pervasive social planning, has firmly entrenched this outlook in our modern perception of the world.

Religious Changes

The role of religion (and particularly national religions) in the agrarian state was largely that of stabilizing and legitimizing the social order. With the rise of the industrial state, however, significant changes have occurred. The church-state alliance has withered, as has the tendency to form national religions. In the industrial society the nationalistic mythologies tend to be secular, political, and sometimes ideological accounts of the national heritage rather than theological or religious statements. The state increasingly exists without religious legitimization in a formal or legal sense. While Robert Bellah and others have pointed to the pervasive nature of "civil religion" in American society and the role it plays in stabilizing our social order, still the fact remains that such social values are not seen by the average American as associated with any particular formal religion or religious institution. Civil religion today therefore plays its role in a fashion somewhat different from that of the religious institutions of agrarian society.

Such a list of changes wrought by industrialization is obviously not exhaustive. In fact, one of the realities of the modern industrial world is its incredible complexity as compared to the agrarian. For our purposes, however, Lenski's characterization of the industrial society will be sufficient to illustrate our central concerns. All that remains before we leave this profile is to note two highly significant social trends evidenced by many modern societies.

The first of these is the reversal of the agrarian tendency toward social inequality.[33] This is not to argue that truly egalitarian ideals now exist, or ever will, but rather that one must use such labels as "ruling class" with far more caution with respect to the industrial society than the agrarian. Power and privilege do exist in the industrial society, but their distribution is a matter substantially more complex today than in the simpler societies of the past (or, one could add, than in the agrarian societies that still exist in the world today).

In this regard it is important to cite several illustrations of the point we are trying to make. We have already alluded to the individualism that characterizes most industrial societies in contrast to the more corporate outlook of the agrarian world. While not all industrial societies exhibit this individualism to the same degree, nonetheless it can be argued that individualism, and indeed a *relative* degree of individual freedom, is in part the result of industrial specialization. The exploding diversity of occupations in our society has been accompanied by a rising vocational freedom and mobility. That this has happened unevenly among the industrialized societies of the world may reflect varying social ideologies and other factors, but the impact of economic individualism on our social perception of reality still remains. Egalitarianism is today a social ideal in a way it never was in the agrarian society.

Yet another illustration of what we are discussing is what is happening to the role and place of women as industrialization spreads. Both Weber and Lenski argue—rightly in our view— that the emancipation of women is at least partly attributable to industrialization.[34] Nor is it hard to see why. The growing economic independence of women today has created both the opportunity and the pressure for egalitarian changes. This correlates well with the situation commented upon earlier with respect to the place of women in agrarian societies. There freedom (and, to a degree, respect) for women was inversely related to one's position on the social scale. Upper-class women were isolated, controlled by social convention, and kept in the home. Lower-class women were forced into the economic system out of sheer necessity and thus were far less isolated than their upper-class sisters. Though it could hardly be argued that these women possessed a social status comparable to males, nonetheless freedom is a relative thing and *some* freedom for lower-class women did exist that upper-class women did not enjoy. The key item is participation in the economic system, and that is why in the industrial society the situation is reversed. Nowadays it is as a woman moves *up* the socioeconomic ladder that more economic participation is possible and hence more freedom gained. As increasing numbers of women in our society achieve economic independence, the trend toward emancipation gathers steam, and with it comes a more outspoken articulation of egalitarian ideals. (The above comments are, of course, *relative*. We are not arguing that women today are free, or that class mobility is possible for all people, only that these things exist to a relatively greater degree than in the agrarian society and, what is more, exist as *ideals* in the industrial society in a way they did not in the agrarian world.)

These comments lead us then to the second noteworthy trend in the industrial state, namely, the tendency for the social class structure to overlap. By this we mean that a person identifiable with one socioeconomic class in the industrial society may nonetheless participate in several other classes simultaneously. A single individual, for example, may own property, be an elected public official, hold a college degree, and be a black female. Any simplistic application of the term "class" to this individual does not do justice to the sociological complexity of her situation.

In the industrial society, class designations are difficult to pin down.[35] Social mobility exists to a greater degree than in the rigid class structure of the agrarian world, and the result is a continual shuffling of our social hierarchies. Kinship ties are looser and class anonymity is more easily achieved. Religion, though it still plays different roles for different segments of society, is nonetheless no longer a primarily urban phenomenon. In some respects today it might be the rural areas that are considered the more religious. Many of the class distinctions between rural and urban populations that were prevalent in agrarian societies no longer pertain. There is, for example, no longer any radical social disapproval of marriage between rural and urban persons.

In the industrial society power and privilege are allocated as the result of many interacting factors: age, race, sex, politics, education, property ownership, vocation, and even geographical location. Out of the mix of these elements, which may even be different for different members of the same family, comes one's place in the social pecking order. It is thus worthwhile to raise the flag of caution about the simplistic use of class terminology in a world as complex as the modern industrial society.

In summary then, we are living today in a society in which the social dynamics are infinitely more complex, and loaded with substantially different freight, than those of the agrarian world. We who live in the industrial society share a social perception of reality that will inevitably incline us to "see" things in the literature of an agrarian culture that would have baffled its authors. We will assign socially sinister or benign meanings where the ancients would have seen none, or miss those self-evident to an agrarian peasant. A single factor such as the ownership of land has a connotation in our world so different from that in agrarian societies that it is hardly surprising when we read meanings into a term like "promised land" that would have been wholly foreign to the authors of the biblical text. This sociologically conditioned knowledge—our social perception of reality —is clearly a part of the preunderstanding we bring to the text and thus a critical dimension of the whole hermeneutical process. With this survey of the agrarian and industrial worlds in front of us, we are moving closer to a position from which we can ask the central hermeneutical question of this entire inquiry: How can we who live in an industrial world read and appropriate the meaning of literary texts written in an agrarian society?

Gaining a Historical Perspective

Before we move to the task of interpretation itself, one additional factor must be taken into account: historical development. Through the three- or four-thousand-year history of their existence, agrarian societies have obviously not remained static in their perception of the world. Though broad generalizations about the movements of social perception are a risky business indeed, if some indications can be given that differentiate developments in broad historical periods, our analysis of the comparative social perception of agrarian and industrial societies will be greatly enhanced.

In a brief but important essay Robert Bellah has attempted to do just this with regard to the religious outlook of the respective societies that have existed up to modern times.[36] The much-heralded claim for a secularistic outlook in contemporary society as compared to the more sacramental view of earlier eras is the kind of thing we are getting at, but for our purposes we need to paint with a much broader brush. We need a view that allows us to see historical development in relation to the macrosociological study we have been doing. An outline of Bellah's work will thus aid us in gaining a sense of historical perspective.

Bellah's essay is entitled "Religious Evolution." Many will be put off by such a rubric, rightly claiming skepticism about evolutionary scenarios that may be shot through with naive or even ideological notions of progress. On the other hand, few would deny that historical development does occur, if not according to some preconceived deterministic scheme, at least in the accidents and events of real human history. In this sense the term "development" perhaps captures better what it is we are looking for, and is in fact what Bellah means by his term "evolution."

Bellah divides this historical development into eras that roughly correspond with the sociological developments we have been discussing. He sees five broad historical eras: primitive, archaic, historic, early modern, and modern. In each he argues for a broadly different, but highly significant, religious outlook.

The first two periods, what are called here the primitive and archaic, when lumped together roughly correspond to what Sjoberg sees as the period of folk societies and what Lenski labels as horticultural. This is the period prior to the rise of agrarian societies and preindustrial cities and thus, depending on geographical location, pushes us back into the third and fourth millennia before Christ. The religion of these two periods is characterized by a fluid system of mythological symbols that presuppose a monistic outlook on reality. Religion and religious practice mimic the thought and action of the gods (nature) and thus serve to promote cosmic harmony and divine favor. Students of the biblical period are familiar with this outlook in much of the religious literature of the Ancient Near East. Such mythology is characterized by a radical identification of the world of nature with human realities such that Bellah speaks of it as a period of *world acceptance,* that is, acceptance of and identification with the natural world as given. The primitive religion of the earlier portion of this period served to reinforce the solidarity of society and to initiate the young into the dance of cosmic harmony. The latter half of the period, what Bellah calls the archaic era, and hence that which immediately preceded the rise of agrarian societies, produced religion that differed little from its predecessor except in a greater emphasis on sacrifice and other cultic practice as a means of currying the favor of the gods. This long period of primitive and archaic societies in which religion was characterized by a radical identification with and acceptance of the world is the first great era from which religious literature has survived.

The shift to what Bellah calls "historic religion" took place with the "emergence in the first millennium B.C. all across the Old World, at least in centers of high culture, of the phenomenon of religious rejection of the world characterized by an extremely negative evaluation of man and society and the exaltation of another realm of reality as alone true and infinitely valuable."[37] This is the period of the agrarian society and is characterized by *world rejection*.

Historic religions share a sense of a transcendent reality that introduces a tension between what is and what should be, hence causing a rejection of the world as it is. Salvation motifs become common, and ideal communities (religious congregations) form. Social perception is thus characterized by a dualism that is at least ethical (Israel), if not cosmological (Persia, Greece).[38] Significantly, it is this sense of reality other than the natural world that for the first time allows a discrete sense of the human self to appear. Human destiny is no longer identical with that of the natural world, and thus a step toward human autonomy has been taken. The human as opposed to the merely natural begins to take on meaning. As Bellah puts it:

> Primitive man could only accept the world in its manifold givenness. Archaic man can through sacrifice fulfill his religious obligations and attain peace with the gods. But the historic religions for the first time promise man that he can understand the fundamental structure of reality and through salvation participate actively in it.[39]

The first pole of the relationship we have been studying then, the agrarian society, is characterized as a period of *world rejection* which, as Weber has noted, arose especially among the lower urban classes.

The third historical era we wish to differentiate is what Bellah calls the "early modern period." It should perhaps not be characterized as a distinct period at all, since it actually functioned as a time of transition between the historic religions and those of the modern world. It is the period roughly corresponding to the Protestant Reformation and was thus on stage as a prelude to the rise of the industrial society. Its chief characteristic is the collapse of the hierarchical structures of both this and the other world. The dualism of the historic period shifts its focus to a confrontation between the transcendent and the human within the arena of ordinary human activity. Salvation is now not a matter of withdrawal from the world but the transformation of it. World rejection is still a dominant motif, but the typical response is moral effort rather than withdrawal. Religious symbols concentrate on the immediacy of the relation between the individual and a transcendent God, while religious action becomes identified with all of life rather than with a few cultic duties. The four-class system (Bellah's description of the agrarian society) begins to break down into the multicentered mode of social organization typical of the industrial society, and both church and state begin to lose their reified character and authority.

When we move into the modern era it becomes increasingly difficult to characterize religion and religious symbol systems. Diversity and complexity are prevalent, but a few trends can be noted that are important to our purposes. The dualism of the historic and early modern periods is disappearing. It is not that we are returning to the monistic view of primitive religions but rather that dualism is being replaced by a multicentered sense of the ground of things. Religious structures in our day are increasingly grounded in the human situation itself and stand as a symbol for the fact that a radical sense of transcendence has withered badly. The modern quest for salvation is in terms of the sense of maturity and well-being of the individual together with the search for a meaningful standard for action in the world. This in turn has led to a view of the endless revisability of both the modern individual and the modern society, a view seen by some as the collapse of moral standards and by others as yet another step toward human autonomy and freedom.

It is worth noting here that Bellah, unlike many contemporary theologians, does not see the developments of the modern era as a process of secularization. Rather he argues that instead of being a "one-possibility thing," life is now an "infinite-possibility thing" in which the symbolization of humankind's relation to the ultimate conditions of existence (which is what Bellah means by religion) is no longer the monopoly of any group or institution labeled religious.

Ours is another great era of *world acceptance*. But this does not imply a simple liberal optimism about the future. The limitations imposed by the human situation have been confronted more deeply in modern times than ever before. It does, however, suggest once again that at the core of the contemporary outlook is the belief that for good or bad the future will be of our own making.

With Bellah's historical scenario now laid out before us in relation to our earlier sociological comparison of agrarian and industrial societies, we perhaps have some basis for our stated concern that the preunderstanding of the interpreter is itself sociologically and historically conditioned, and that this conditioning will provide examples of both consanguinity and disjunction between text and interpreter that we must take into account. No one could seriously argue that the brush of history paints so cleanly as to cover up the strokes of earlier eras, so that many of the motifs of earlier religious and social perceptions are still with us today. In many ways this historical residue is very much alive and must be dealt with, yet it is also true that much of our social perception of reality today is truly unique and cannot be glossed over. We would not want to claim that theological meanings of earlier eras are no longer valid for us. If none were, the Bible could be quietly laid to rest on the shelf of history. What we are attempting to say is that efforts to understand the biblical text today require every possible means of allowing the text to speak in its own context so that it can be more clearly heard in ours. It is the clarity of the gospel that is our concern—that it be permitted once again to lay hold of us and create for us the event of the Good News. In the hope of enhancing that process for the preacher, by acknowledging the sociological and historical conditioning of our preunderstanding, it is now time to turn to the biblical text itself.

4

Interpretation in a Sociological Context
1 Kings 21:1-29

In the context of discussing the appropriate methodology for interpreting the parables of Jesus, Dan Otto Via, Jr., comments: "In the hands of some of its practitioners the historical approach threatens to leave the parables in the past with nothing to say to the present."[1] A hermeneutical method limited to historical-critical questions would do exactly that and is therefore not enough.[2] Via then adds: "Seeking the [historical] life setting does not in itself restrict a parable to the past. The question is what the next hermeneutical step must be."[3] Exactly! Unlike the first hearers of the biblical message, the interpreter in our day is required to live in two worlds at once. He must learn to live first in the world of the text itself, becoming in whatever small measure it is possible to do so a contemporary of its authors and first hearers. He must learn its language and begin to hear the echoes that reverberate behind its scenes. Its people, its habits of life, and something of the implications that lie hidden between its lines must all become a part of the interpreter's consciousness if he is to claim to be able to say anything of what the text once meant.

But we must also say what the text means—now in our own day.[4] That is, what would otherwise be a purely historical exercise must also become a *theological* one if the text is to say anything normative for us now. Yet it is precisely here—in the attempt to say what the text means now—that the hermeneutical enterprise is in trouble. The interpreter of today must live not only in the biblical world but also in his own world—open to the dilemmas and struggles required in this particular time and place if one is to inquire about the ultimate conditions and meaning of human existence. Only one who possesses more than a superficial perception of the meaning of his own time has any real means of communicating at the depth theology requires. Yet our problem has historically been that, living as we must with a foot in both the biblical world and that of our own day, we have too easily assumed statements about the one to be statements about the other. Historical statements have become confused with theological statements, and texts have been made to say what their historical meaning does not warrant. Right here is the nub of the hermeneutical problem in our day and the reason clarity is needed as we take the next step.

As one part of a next step in the interpretive process, we propose taking the studies we have done of agrarian and industrial societies and using what help they can give in that effort to live simultaneously in the two worlds of the biblical interpreter. By using these studies as background, let us see if we can to any degree both clarify and enrich the pathway between what a selected biblical text once meant and what it now means. We shall look in some detail at both Old and New Testament passages as illustrations of our claim for the value of sociology in seeking the common ground (as well as the lack thereof) between ourselves and the text. While numerous passages (presumably) could be used as illustrations, it is methodology and not commentary that is our primary concern, and we judge that it will therefore be of more value to deal with a few passages in some detail than with a wide variety in a superficial manner.

Our methodology in dealing with each text chosen for study will involve several steps.

1. Appropriate historical-critical notations must be made to ensure that the text is set in its proper *Sitz im Leben* and that the language is understood in light of the appropriate historical referents.

2. As an additional step in attempting to say what the text *meant*, we shall then run it through the grid of sociological data developed in our studies of the agrarian world.

3. As a first step in clarifying what the text *means* for our day, we shall begin by looking at what it has been said to mean by contemporary preachers and interpreters. Here we shall be looking primarily for proclamatory and homiletical statements, since it is this final step in the hermeneutical process—preaching—that is our main concern.

4. In the attempt to sharpen and clarify what are truly appropriate interpretations for our own day, we shall then use the profiles of both the agrarian and industrial societies to critique the homiletical contributions cited above. Our purpose will be not only to ask about their adequacy in light of the agrarian background of the text, but also to comment upon the conditioning they evidence that may be the result of having been developed in an industrial setting.

5. Finally, we shall draw from each of our examples what conclusions we may about the sociological consanguinity (or lack thereof) between ourselves and the text that might guide us in bringing the text to execution in our own day. Since any text has in it a variety of theological leads that may be followed by the preacher, our purpose will not be to assume there is one and only one definitive way to use the text today. Rather, we hope to give examples of the transpositions that are necessary in following these leads in order that the sermon bear faithful relation to the intention of the text.

With these methodological steps in front of us, let us turn to the first of the texts we have chosen for comment.

1 Kings 21:1–29

The Old Testament text we have chosen for study is the story of Naboth's vineyard in 1 Kings 21:1–29. We have done so because it raises the issue of property and proprietary rights and therefore deals with one of those human concerns looked at very differently in the agrarian and industrial worlds. It also happens to be a text that, by virtue of coming out of a sociological context quite different from that of contemporary America, has suffered badly in the transition from text to sermon.

The story in 1 Kings 21:1–29 is a simple one. Ahab, the king of Israel, wished to purchase a vineyard belonging to a fellow named Naboth, a Jezreelite. Jezreel being but a short distance from the palace of Ahab at Samaria, the vineyard had apparently caught the king's attention and he wished to own it for himself. In spite of a fair offer from Ahab, however, Naboth refused either to sell the land or exchange it for another piece. Ahab, upset at not getting his way, returned home, pouted with his face to the wall, and refused to eat.

This Ahab, who the writer of 1 Kings informs us did more to provoke the anger of the Lord than all the kings of Israel before him,[5] is thus discovered by his Phoenician wife, Jezebel, in a state of mental depression. Reacting with the typical agrarian assumptions about proprietary privilege, Jezebel then arranges to have false charges brought against Naboth, has him stoned to death, and finally informs Ahab that the vineyard is his for the taking. As Ahab goes to acquire his property he is confronted by the prophet Elijah, who pronounces upon him and all his male heirs a curse of death. Jezebel too is placed under a grisly curse while Ahab, on hearing of his fate, repents in sackcloth and humbles himself before God. As a result of this repentance the doom of Ahab's house is postponed for one generation.[6]

We have agreed that, before turning to efforts at interpreting this story in our own society, it is necessary to use the historical-critical data to set it in its proper *Sitz im Leben*. It is thus appropriate to remind ourselves of the historical setting of the book of 1 Kings itself. Using earlier compilations of records kept in the royal archives, the palace, and the Temple, together with collections of stories about Elijah and Elisha that had circulated in both oral and written form, an unknown author in about the year 600 B.C. worked this traditional material into a literary and theological framework that produced a first edition of our books of 1 and 2 Kings. This writer appears to have worked after the death of Josiah (608 B.C.) but before the invasion of Judah in 597 B.C., and apparently belonged to that deuteronomic school of reformers that was also responsible for Joshua, Judges, and the two books of Samuel.

It is also probable that this first edition of 1 and 2 Kings underwent further revision after the disastrous events that led to the destruction of Jerusalem and the first deportation to Babylon. Since the last date referred to in the two-volume work is 561 B.C. (2 Kings 25:27), it can be assumed that this further deuteronomic redaction of the books took place some time after that date and before the return of the exiles in 538 B.C.

This places the book firmly within the agrarian world of which we have been speaking. The cities of that period, including Jerusalem and Samaria, were the preindustrial cities of which Sjoberg speaks. Moreover, being located in the middle of the first millennium B.C., the events of 1 Kings fall squarely into the era Robert Bellah has labeled the "historic period." It may be remembered that this was a period of what Bellah called world rejection or, as we might put it, a period of tension between the world as it is and the world as envisioned by an external ethical standard.

Next we may note that within our text there are clear signs of deuteronomic redaction. Verses 25–26 obviously interject the typical deuteronomic formula of rewards and punishments, as does the speech of Elijah in verses 20b–22 and 24. It has been suggested that the latter is the work of the original deuteronomic compiler of the narrative (ca. 600 B.C.) and that the former, verses 25–26, are the work of the later redactor who sought to leave no doubt about his evaluation of Ahab.[7]

Verse 23 also seems to interrupt the flow of the story and could be a later addition, although it does match well with the general tenor of the Deuteronomist's attitude toward Jezebel.

In his mind she was a clear threat to the purity of Israel.[8]   Indeed, it is plain in the story that Jezebel and not Ahab (note Ahab's repentance) is the archvillain, perhaps reflecting the Deuteronomist's fear that syncretistic influences from the outside would make Israel just another Canaanite state.   Deuteronomist influence is perhaps also seen in the careful notation in verse 13 that there were two witnesses to the supposed crime of Naboth just as prescribed by the deuteronomic tradition.[9]

Several smaller critical notes can also be made that will contribute something to our understanding of the text.   The title given to Ahab in verse 1 is "king of Samaria."   John Gray takes this odd usage to reflect the situation of crown possession of Samaria as the basis for the power of the house of Omri.[10]   If this is so, proprietary property rights are involved.   By contrast, we note that the exclamation ḥālīlāh ("God forbid!") in verse 3 implies that Ahab's proposal to Naboth was wrong in the eyes of God as well as those of Naboth's family.

The term ḥorîm is an interesting one as well. It means "freeborn" in most Semitic languages but in Hebrew it is better translated "nobility."[11]   That is to say, we are dealing in this story with the political-military elite we identified earlier in our study of the agrarian society.   Moreover, the letter-writing campaign of Jezebel to the nobility of Jezreel makes sense only if we assume the kinship ties that usually caused the agrarian upper classes to close ranks when threatened.   Thus if it is correct to read ḥorîm as referring to the landed nobility of Jezreel, their ready acquiescence in Jezebel's scheme comes immediately clear. They were acting like the typical agrarian political-military elite which, as Lenski has noted, participated with the crown in the prerogatives of rulership.

In verse 12 we are told that a fast was proclaimed and Naboth set "on high among the people."   Gray suggests that Naboth, *being also a part of this landed aristocracy,* would have been accustomed to being a spokesman in Jezreel and having his voice heard.[12]   His place at the head of a conference among the local nobility thus lends an air of decorum and fairness to the proceedings. The fast, which is an act of cultic significance, provides the proper sense of religious legitimation to what is to follow, not unlike the way prayers of invocation are used in our society before football games or meetings of the local PTA. Naboth's challenge to the crown, however, was not expected publicly and may have surprised Jezebel, who might have thought that placing Naboth under the peer pressure of the council of nobles would inhibit a public challenge to the crown. In any case, Jezebel was prepared with two witnesses against Naboth, and their testimony is a clear example of the political use of cultic prescriptions to legitimate what was going on.[13] In Deuteronomy 17:6 we read: "On the evidence of two witnesses or of three witnesses he that is to die shall be put to death; a person shall not be put to death on the evidence of one witness." When the two witnesses speak to condemn Naboth they are quickly supported by their peers in a typical closing of rank among the elite class. Jezebel obviously understood that this is exactly what would happen.

With these brief historical-critical notes in mind, it is now possible to attempt a summary of the passage from within the context of agrarian sociology. Ahab appears to be making an attempt to assume the usual (at least outside Israel) proprietary rights of agrarian monarchs which, in the Deuteronomist's mind, is clearly in violation of Israel's covenant with Yahweh. He doubtless saw it as the inevitable consequence of having opened the doors to the evil institution of monarchy. After the corrupting influence of the dynasties of Jeroboam and Baasha, what could one now expect except just such a progressive deterioration of the commitment to Yahweh as Israel's only true king? That this is the Deuteronomist's judgment of the matter is clear from the redaction noted above.

The question of Jezebel to Ahab, "Do you now govern Israel?" makes it clear that she assumes the royal prerogatives as would any agrarian ruler. She is puzzled that Ahab would not. The fact that Ahab pouts when Naboth refuses to give up the land suggests his (or the redactor's) knowledge that expropriation of land was a direct violation of the covenant and not among the king's prerogatives in Israel's theocratic state. The agrarian idea that "the king is god," which is the final conclusion of any attempt at religious legitimation of the existing social order, is precisely what Israel had rejected in the covenants of Sinai and Shechem. What is thus at stake is *far more than a piece of land; it is the fundamental nature of the covenant with Yahweh.* The Israelite covenantal affirmation that "God is king" is being challenged by the conventional wisdom of the agrarian state, which assumes the opposite. Moreover, given this fact, the actions of Jezebel in the story make perfect sense. Not only does she anticipate that the nobles of Jezreel will come to her support, but she also realizes that the weak (apparently) reaction of Ahab threatens more than simply to prevent the acquisition of a desired piece of property. It threatens the entire sociopolitical structure of which Ahab and Jezebel are a part. "Naboth cursed God *and the king*" is the charge. In the agrarian state the one is not separate from the other. Naboth was thus challenging the religious legitimation of the state in a way that Jezebel understood far more clearly than Ahab. By the same token, from the prophetic (Elijah's) point of view the issue was also much larger than a small plot of land. The covenant with Yahweh was at stake.

The small plot of land, however, should not be forgotten. The land in Israel was a tangible sign of the covenant. It was *promised* land, and did not cease to be such after it was occupied. Naboth's exclamation *hālilāh* implies exactly this. Naboth (or again, the redactor) knows full well that the land is not his to sell or trade. It is the family's covenant heritage and not his alone. But even beyond that, the land is God's. He has given it to Israel (and to Naboth's family) in sacred trust as the fulfillment of the promise, and therefore to alter the status of the land would be to tamper with the covenant itself.

It should be clear from our summary so far that the theological orientation of Israel was atypical of the ordinary agrarian state. The covenant with Yahweh that the deuteronomic redactor of our text tries valiantly to defend was in many respects incompatible with the usual agrarian social pattern. Elijah the prophet, the one who speaks the word of the Lord, makes this crystal clear. The sentence Elijah pronounces upon Ahab and Jezebel is, of course, the expected deuteronomic outcome of the story: evil is punished and righteousness rewarded. But perhaps it is also legitimate to suggest that the grisly nature of the punishments and their ultimate fulfillment in the story are a clue to the Deuteronomist's assessment of the seriousness of the crime. Dogs, the scavengers of every preindustrial city (Is there cryptic symbolism here? Are the scavengers an ironic symbol of the scavenger or outcast status of the early Hebrews who formed the covenant at Sinai? Have we come full circle in the grisly end of Ahab and his Queen?), lick the blood and eat the flesh of Ahab and Jezebel. As the pair sought to devour, so they have been devoured. The covenant with Yahweh has been restored with grim vengeance.

Elijah can now be seen to be playing the proper and typical role of Israelite prophets. He is not rebuking Ahab for some private sin, for having fallen prey to the temptation of greed, he is calling Ahab, and indeed all Israel, to recognize and return to the Sinai covenant. If Jezebel's actions in the story indicate how clearly she understood what was at stake from the perspective of the ordinary agrarian monarch, so Ahab's fearful vacillation and eventual remorse make clear from the covenant perspective that he too knows on what dangerous ground he treads. He has come perilously close to assuming the prerogative of God.

In summary it is possible to assert that a knowledge of the sociology of agrarian societies has greatly illumined the meaning of at least this particular biblical text. By adding the sociological perspective to that of the usual historical-critical study, we have perhaps come a bit closer to understanding what the text meant to say in its own place and time. For both the original compiler and later redactor of this text, it identified clearly the reason for the great calamities that befell Israel in the sixth century B.C. Israel had forsaken the covenant with Yahweh. The sociological roles of Naboth, the Jezreelite nobility, and Ahab and his foreign queen all help to clarify the way in which the religious issue of Yahweh's sovereignty played itself out in the real lives of real people.

With these understandings now in hand, however, we must take the next step in the hermeneutical process: asking what the text means in the industrial world of our own day. As we do so we are immediately confronted with questions about the sociology of our knowledge in the present day. If we are going to attempt to bring the text's original message to execution now, especially as that is done in preaching, we are going to have to inquire about how our present-day social perception of reality will or will not let us hear the text on its own terms. Our discussion of this matter will be given higher graphic relief if we follow our announced method of turning next to ways in which this text has in fact been used by preachers in our industrial society.

If it were not so tragic it would almost be funny to be confronted with the way this text of 1 Kings 21 has been handled by preachers in this century in this society. One need not look for extreme examples of shoddy exegesis to see the problem; respected preachers and popular interpreters amply demonstrate the concern.

Dr. Ralph Sockman, for many years a distinguished writer, speaker, and pastor (of Christ Church, New York City), has written the expository section of *The Interpreter's Bible* on the text of 1 Kings 21:1–29.[14] He has chosen to focus his homiletical interpretation on the subject of "selling one's soul."

> Ahab sold his soul for the price of his neighbor's vineyard. Our minds are arrested by the thought of selling our souls outright

as in this case, or as did Faust in the familiar legend, or as George Eliot's Silas Marner sold his soul for a pile of gold, or as did Cardinal Wolsey for political power.[15]

He goes on:

Some hold that if we would stress, as did our grandfathers, the dread punishment for such sinners, we could restrain the current trends to evil. But one wonders whether it is the severity of the punishment or the subtlety of the selling which needs to be watched and emphasized.[16]

In light of our discussion above, one has to wonder what in the world all this has to do with the text in 1 Kings. But Sockman continues, discussing how we can sell our souls in small and subtle ways:

In the presence of some people we cannot call our souls our own, because we have done things which keep us from being our true selves. Consider the minister of the Gospel. As a minister he is ordained to preach the word of God as sincerely as he can know it. But he asks himself, "What good is it to proclaim God's word if I have few who hear it? Must I not give my message in such a way that it will win acceptance by my people?"[17]

Sockman then explains that in compromising the truth such a pastor has sold his soul subtly but surely. The whole discussion then ends with exhortations to put first things first.

Such commentary seems ludicrous at best. And we say that not in order to be overly caustic to Sockman, who was obviously a victim of the state of the hermeneutical art when and where he wrote (New York City, 1954), but to point out how obviously the social conditioning of Sockman's preunderstanding has shaped his interpretation of the text. No doubt Ahab was morally culpable of personal shortcomings, but it is clear from our earlier discussion that it is not so much the character of Ahab, bad as that may have been, that is at issue. It is the institution of monarchy and the threat inherent in it to supplant the lordship of Yahweh. Ahab is a bad actor, but in the Deuteronomist's mind Ahab was no more or no less than what was to be expected from the corrupting influences of monarchical power and

Canaanite religion. It is Jezebel and what she represents that is the crux of the matter, not Ahab.

One is almost forced to ask at this point about the sociology of Sockman's knowledge that led to such an open disregard for the historical and sociological context of the story. We need to ask if it is possible to draw any conclusions from the fact that Sockman did his interpreting in the context of the modern industrial society, and if such conclusions might help us avoid this use of a text to discuss unrelated issues. Armed with at least some awareness of the relation between the context of the interpreter and the context of the text, perhaps we can move closer to genuine dialogue with the biblical message.

It seems probable that Sockman did not know the background of the agrarian world that we have summarized above. If he did, he chose to disregard it, but the probability is that he did not. The historical-critical notes done by Norman Snaith that are a part of the volume of *The Interpreter's Bible* in which Sockman wrote were available to him, however, and while they are far from exhaustive they do make at least a few suggestions in the direction we have outlined above.

Why did Sockman choose to ignore them? Perhaps the answer is to be found in the sociological context of Sockman's pulpit. In New York City in 1954, who knew or cared anything about the proprietary rights of agrarian kings? Or, for that matter, who else in the industrial society of today knows or cares? We have no monarchy, no proprietary rights, no landed aristocracy (at least not in quite the same way that it existed in the agrarian world), no *promised* land, and so on. How then are we to understand the text?

Sockman turned the text into a moralistic, individualistic exhortation to be nicer people. In the industrial society of New York City he would have had a difficult time tying the text to the issues of social class, internecine struggles among members of the agrarian elite, and the theocratic covenant with Yahweh. But unless *some* means can be found to do exactly this, it would be difficult to argue that the text has anything to say to the industrial world. Left to interpret this text without building a bridge to the sociology of the agrarian society, the preacher of today, like Ralph Sockman, easily allows the sermon to become an escape from social relevance into a purely individualistic piety.

If we thus cannot argue that Sockman was in touch with the agrarian world of the text in 1 Kings, we surely ought to be able to assert that he was in touch with the world in which he lived. In addition to the large congregation that he served, he spoke regularly to millions of Americans on radio broadcasts and every month sent out over twenty-five thousand newsletters to people who listened to him. His correspondence with these listeners was of staggering proportions. Almost certainly Sockman was right in assuming that a sermon encouraging individuals to guard the integrity of their souls would have been easily understood by the audience for whom he wrote. Sharing the individualistic bias of industrial societies, and assuming as does our era that religion addresses the well-being and maturity of the individual,[18] this is exactly what his hearers would have been able to understand. The world rejection, and consequent ethical tension, of Israelite society was played out in the corporate issues of social class struggle, national idolatry, and the relation of the whole people to Yahweh. But taking a reading from his industrialized society, Sockman (consciously or unconsciously) has transposed this into a message about the moral character of the individual.

Though the text in 1 Kings is plainly about the idolatrous role of the elite, and thus addresses the peculiar role and temptations of this group, Sockman makes no mention of social class whatever. Perhaps he does not because in the industrial society the sharp and rigid class distinctions of the agrarian world do not pertain and therefore the issue was never raised to consciousness for him. That Sockman is in many ways typical of the preachers of this society is unfortunately all too true. *Most* of us would probably have difficulty identifying the class issues involved in the 1 Kings text, precisely because we share Sockman's sociologically conditioned preunderstanding.

Finally then, having criticized Sockman's attempt to bring to faithful execution the intention of our text, we must ask ourselves what is required if we are not to continue turning this story into a moral for better living among the middle-class Protestants of the industrial world. We need to ask how one translates the sociological, *and hence theological,* issues of the text into the language and perception of our own time.

To do this, in our judgment, requires finding aspects of the sociological situation in the industrial society that bear some consanguinity with those we have highlighted in the text. We do not claim that this is *all* that is required—we are not attempting to rule out of court the existential search for consanguinity made by Bultmann—but rather that the sociological loading of texts such as those we have chosen requires *some* effort at finding a common sociological ground.

Since every preacher's sociological context will be slightly different from that of every other preacher, and since any text may lend itself to a variety of theological interpretations, we cannot presume to have uncovered the definitive interpretation of 1 Kings 21:1–29.[19] It occurs to us, however, that several key questions are unavoidable. If, for example, the covenant with Yahweh is inextricably tied to land (which in our own editorial judgment it is), where or what is the land of promise now? If it is plausible to argue that since the coming of Christ the whole earth now qualifies for that title, who is buying, selling, or trading it in violation of the covenant? Where in the industrial society are the issues of social idolatry and the sovereignty of God now being played out? Who, in relation to our fluid and complex class structures, might be considered the upper classes about whom this kind of story could be told? In an era that neither wants nor needs religious legitimation of the state from a specific institution such as the Christian church, how is this legitimation now achieved? Who is involved in the process, that is, who plays the role of Jezebel? Should we follow Ivan Illich's suggestion and apply the text to the role of the public school teacher? Surely he is right that the schools play a major role in sanctioning the status quo in this country. Would Robert Bellah's concept of "civil religion" offer insight into how these things work in our day?

Unless these questions or something like them can lead us to common ground with the sociological background of the text in 1 Kings, it would be difficult to see much integrity in its use in the pulpit. If the purpose of the text was originally that of forcing decision, yes or no, for or against a social claim to ultimacy, and if that same decision is to confront us today as the text's theological or normative demand upon us, then sermons encouraging us as individuals to be nicer people will not make it. The radical quality of the text's demand upon us will have completely disappeared.

No doubt if we were to speak the same message that is proclaimed in 1 Kings 21 today, in the same radical fashion that the text once declared it, we would be no more popular than was Elijah when he spoke to Ahab and Jezebel. Yet it is in precisely those places where the elite of any society assume the prerogative of God that the word of the Lord must be most radically declared. Here the step in the hermeneutical process that moves beyond the purely historical questions about what the text once meant, to the theological questions about what it now means, demands the search either for common ground or for the means of transposition to let the text speak on its own terms. Bultmann's categories of individualistic existential analysis are one such search, but in a text such as that we have been discussing they would prove inadequate. Nor would the text be completely served by Bultmann's notion that preunderstanding is universal in scope and thus the interpretations to which it leads us can be universally applied. Preunderstanding is *always* conditioned both historically and sociologically. Highlighting this conditioning in the situation of the text *and the interpreter* is a step toward clarifying both ends of the hermeneutical chain. It also gives us the means to relate them. In that effort, at least in relation to 1 Kings 21, the works of Gerhard Lenski, Gideon Sjoberg, Peter Berger, Max Weber, and other sociologists of religion are probably of more value to us than Faust, Silas Marner, or Cardinal Wolsey.

5

Parables in a Sociological Context
Luke 16:19-31

The parables of Jesus bring together two different kinds of human experience: that of the ordinary world of everyday affairs and that of a universe of reflective meaning by which we seek to articulate for ourselves the significance of what is going on. These are the two worlds Berger and Luckmann labeled the "reality of everyday experience" and a "province of finite meaning," the latter being a plane of perception that temporarily lifts the curtain on a stage to reveal the tension which exists between its vision of the meaning of human life and that which exists in the plane of everyday reality. The parable is thus an experience in comparison—carrying our attention by means of the unexpected twists and turns of the story to see the relation between our ordinary lives and the normative claims or existential decisions the parable wishes to place before us. Parables are therefore an ideal occasion for the type of analysis in which we are interested: that of relating theological meaning to the social perception of the world.

The particular parable we have chosen for comment is that found in Luke 16:19-31. It is usually called the parable of the Rich Man and Lazarus. We have chosen it for several reasons, not the least of which is the fact that it involves clear distinctions of social class that will give us reason to ask if interpreters in our industrial world have picked up this obvious fact, and if not, why not. The fact that this parable appears only in Luke will also help to focus our study by simplifying the task of relating this particular pericope to the history of the synoptic tradition. Moreover, lacking comparative synoptic material for analysis places greater importance on the internal Lucan context of our text and its relation to the larger sweep of Luke's theology. As we shall see in a moment, these latter concerns will be directly addressed by the sociological perspective we have chosen to highlight and will have a major bearing on the interpretation of the passage.

It has been agreed in our methodology that we must begin with the appropriate historical-critical notes that can give us perspective on the text's life situation. This will be especially important with our present text because different views of the historical background of the pericope have led scholars to widely divergent views of the parable's meaning.

Prior to any attempt to state the meaning of a synoptic text, it is the usual habit of New Testament scholarship to try to trace back the history of the text's transmission in the early Christian community in order to isolate, if possible, the earliest form the text may have had. Only when this has been done can the text be assigned a setting (and thus an origin) in either the life of Jesus, the life of the early church, or the surrounding cultural milieu. In the case of Luke 16:19–31 this history of tradition is both significant and fascinating.

Virtually all commentators have seen that this parable has two parts: (1) verses 19–26, which describe a reversal of fortunes in the world to come, and (2) verses 27–31, which assert the uselessness of miracles like resurrection of the dead in evoking belief.[1] Thus we are faced not only with the problem of the origin of the two parts but also with the problem of the relation between them. Both issues are significant for our eventual interpretation.

Since the writing of a detailed monograph on this parable in 1918 by Hugo Gressmann, it has been customary for scholars to find the source of verses 19–26 in the Egyptian story of the journey of Si-Osiris, the son of Setme Chamois, to the under-

70

world.[2] That story concludes: "He who has been good on earth, will be blessed in the kingdom of the dead."[3] This story, which suggests a reversal of fortunes much like that in our text, Joachim Jeremias believes was brought to Palestine by Alexandrian Jews where a version of the story became popular as the tale of a poor scholar and a rich publican.[4] Frank W. Beare notes that as many as seven rabbinic versions of the story have existed as well.[5] Thus it has been suggested that Jesus drew on folkloric material that was already well-known, gave to it his own twist, and then added the material in verses 27–31 in order to make his own unique point.[6] Bultmann rejects this notion and assigns both halves of the story to Jewish sources that have been put into the mouth of Jesus by the early church.[7] He sees the first part of the story as teaching the usual Jewish doctrine of rewards and punishments, while the second half is seen as merely echoing a familiar Jewish idea that miracles do not elicit belief, that only the Scriptures can do that.[8] *Why* the early Christian community might then have chosen to incorporate this Jewish theology into the teachings of Jesus, Bultmann does not say, and, indeed, one can wonder if *Gentile* literature such as Luke's Gospel would really be the only synoptic repository of this story were Bultmann's view correct.

Still others have suggested that one or the other of the two parts of the story is attributable to Jesus but not its totality. Thus John Crossan argues that it is the first half of the story that is from Jesus, though shorn of its moralistic doctrine of rewards and punishments (note that nothing in the story actually implies a moral judgment of either key figure), while the second half can be wholly attributed to the Easter faith of the early church.[9] Our own view, however, is that Joachim Jeremias is correct, that both halves of the story can be attributed to Jesus, the former because it *is* different from the usual Jewish theology of rewards and punishments (the point Bultmann missed), and the latter because, as we shall point out in more detail later, resurrection *is not* what the story is about.[10] Even though the allusion to resurrection in the story may reflect concerns of the early church, the main thrust of the parable is not in this direction and can properly be attributed to Jesus himself.

That this judgment is plausible can be seen if we set the story in its internal Lucan context. It appears in a chapter in which the use of wealth is the major concern. Verses 14–15 introduce the subject of the love of money and the use of it to justify one's social and moral position. There too the theme of the reversal of fortunes is broached, a theme that appears in Luke's version of the birth of Jesus as well as in his account of Jesus' teaching on the plain of Capernaum.[11] Whether this concern for the condition of the poor is attributable only to Luke and not to Jesus is difficult to say, but it is at least consistent with Jesus as portrayed throughout Luke's work. It is also in accord with the Jesus presented to us in the other synoptic Gospels. Moreover, the second theme of our parable, the value of the Scriptures, is likewise introduced by the context in verses 16–18. It too is consistent with the synoptic portrayal of Jesus as the One who came not to destroy the law but to fulfill it.

Of perhaps key significance is the latter half of the parable and its possible attribution to Jesus. Jeremias has pointed to the fact that in the double-edged parables of Jesus it is the latter point that is the key to understanding what the whole parable is about.[12] If Jesus has thus taken a bit of folklore and turned it to his own use (as we are arguing), it will be in this latter section of the story that Jesus' meaning will be found. Both Jeremias and J. M. Creed have rightly noted that, as the second section of the parable makes clear, the character of Lazarus is an incidental one in the story.[13] It is the Rich Man *and his five brothers* who are of central concern. The notion that no miracle is needed to authenticate what the Scriptures have made plain is also incidental to the *main point*: the warning to the Rich Man and his subsequent concern that his brothers be warned and thus saved from the fate that has befallen him. The brothers, like the Rich Man before his death, are those of whom Jesus speaks in verse 15: "You [who are lovers of money] are those who justify yourselves before men." The message of the parable is thus addressed to the rich and their self-justifying ways, a message that is readily attributable to Jesus' peculiar situation, whatever use may have been made of this story by the early church.[14]

The line of reasoning that we are following seems justified from the Lucan context that follows our text as well. The discussions of gratitude and forgiveness in 17:1–19 are followed by a series of eschatological sayings, which in turn lead to yet another story of the reversal of values and judgment (the Tax Collector and the Pharisee) that Jesus is bringing. The next section, 18:18–30 (the parable of the Rich Young Man), repeats the warning about the morally self-justifying tendencies of the rich and acts as a preface to Jesus' prediction of his death. That is to say, Luke has 16:19–31 in the eschatological context of the coming kingdom. The advent of a new day in which the reversal of judgment and value will be a reality is fast breaking in. The time is short. And that is why parables giving warning about the decisive character of the moment are placed here by Luke. They fit well with Luke's overall perception of the "new age" in the salvation-history of the world. Our text is neither an unreconstructed statement of the Jewish concern for the law and the prophets (Bultmann), nor a graphic description of life after death (Beare), but an eschatological warning to the rich that what was heralded at Jesus' birth—"He has filled the hungry with good things, and the rich he has sent empty away" (Luke 1:53)—is about to come into being. The text is an eschatological warning about the coming of the new age.

Before we move into a consideration of what light our sociological perspective may be able to shed on this particular text, we must take quick note of several other critical items that will help us understand. In verse 20 the cripple is given the name Lazarus (the only figure in the parables who is named), meaning "God helps." While some commentators have tried to draw doubtful associations with the Lazarus of John 11, the more likely significance of the name here is in seeing it over against the outlook of late Judaism that counted earthly miseries as evidence of divine punishment for sin. Both Lazarus's name and the eventual outcome of the story thus represent incongruities between the attitude of Jesus and that of his listeners. Jesus is *not* merely echoing the doctrine of rewards and punishments.

Several touches in the story emphasize the gulf between Lazarus and the Rich Man (often called "Dives" from the Vulgate's use of that Latin term to translate *plousias*). The Rich Man, who had no need to work and feasted every day, was attired in a costly mantle of purple wool and fine Egyptian linen underwear. Lazarus, by contrast, is a cripple, reduced to begging, who receives bread thrown from the tables of the rich. The bread is not crumbs. The rich of that day used bread to wipe their hands after dining and then threw it under the table or out the window. It is this condition of extreme social disparity between the two main characters that is then reversed in the strongest possible terms in the latter part of the story when Lazarus is said to rest on the bosom of Abraham, the place of honor among the righteous.[15]

We should also note that verses 22–31 are concerned not with the final state but with the state immediately after death. This is indicated by the use of the term *hadēs* as distinct from *geenna*.[16] The notion that in the intermediate state the righteous and wicked can see one another and converse has parallels in both apocryphal and rabbinic sources. Caution about using this kind of material for discussions of the conditions of life after death should be evident, however, both from the fact that Jesus is using folkloric material here that is drawn from popular sources and from the fact that this type of material is virtually unique to this text in all the synoptic literature.

The only other item of a critical nature that need concern us is to note that the text lacks significant textual variations with the doubtful exception of that in verse 31, which has led some scholars to argue a case for the redactive influence of the early church on the text: "If, as is probable, *anastē* be the original reading the resurrection of Jesus (or of Lazarus, cf. Jo. xi.) and the subsequent unbelief of the Jews can hardly have been absent from the mind of the evangelist."[17] It is this that has led Crossan to see strong ties between our text and the resurrection account of Luke 24, causing him to reject the latter half of the story as genuine.[18] Since the textual alternatives do not significantly alter the thrust of the verse, however, and since the whole matter of resurrection is not the thrust of the text, this argument strikes us as tangential at best. It is indeed possible to see a polemic against the refusal of the Jews to believe in verse 31, and the matter does indeed call to mind the resurrection of Jesus, but to see this as more than incidental to the text (even though the text may have been used by the early church for these reasons) destroys both the central point of the passage and the unity between the two halves of the story. It is only if the latter section is interpreted as a warning to the rich of the impending new age that the earlier section about the reversal of fortunes has any reason for being in the text at all. And it is precisely the failure to see this point that has led interpreters (Bultmann, Beare, Crossan) to designate one part of the story or the other as unrelatable to the specific context of the ministry of Jesus.

It is time now, however, to move on to the next step. We must ask if our sociological perspective on agrarian societies can add or clarify anything in this discussion of what the text once meant. Here it will be our contention that the sociological insight we can bring to the story will confirm the line of interpretation we have already begun to develop, namely, that the central thrust of the parable is a warning to the rich that the new age is upon them, and that Jeremias is right in asserting that it should properly be named the parable of the Six Brothers.[19]

To begin, we must note the sociological characterizations of the Rich Man and Lazarus at which the text hints. The Rich

Man is said to wear the costly garments and live the luxurious life-style of the upper classes. It is perhaps impossible to decide from the brief material in the text whether he was from the military-political group or the cultural-religious elite, but he is clearly from the upper strata of society. It can also be surmised that the setting of the story is the preindustrial city, because it was in the center of such cities that the rich lived.

The fact that this Rich Man's immediate concern on finding out his eventual plight is to take it all as a threat to his family is typical of both groups, but perhaps especially of the political-military elite, which had both close and widespread family ties. Even at such a late date in his own personal crisis as that portrayed in our story, the Rich Man takes no thought whatever for either Lazarus or the plight of those like him who remain alive. The fact that he thinks only of his peers is one of the parable's more telling points, and having been phrased this way by Jesus, the parable could represent his skepticism about the ability of the rich to hear such a message at all. The rich, as always in the agrarian society, are concerned only to justify their own position and to protect that of their peers who make the system work. One can even imagine the nodding heads of the poor among Jesus' hearers who listened to him tell this story and recognized a pattern they had seen over and over again.

Since it is the actions of the Rich Man—his unremitting concern for himself and his kin—that constitute the heart of the story, it is plausible to argue that a believable setting in the life of Jesus for this story can be found in his frequent attacks on the apathy and indifference of the rich. Jesus is warning persons who resemble the Rich Man. Presumably the audience would then have included just such persons as the appropriate addressees, while Lazarus (and the poor in the audience) is really a secondary figure in the story introduced to clarify other aspects of Jesus' meaning we shall comment on shortly. It is the rich, the indifferent, the upper classes symbolized by the story's central character, who are the main concern.

Lazarus is poor, there is no doubt about that. He is, in fact, one of those persons outside the usual sociological characterizations of the social classes of the preindustrial city, and therefore the term "poor" cannot be applied to him without further considerations. He belongs neither to that class of urban poor that made up the bulk of the city population (merchants, artisans, craftsmen), nor to the rural poor we usually call peasants, but to the relatively small group of outcasts that inhabited the gutters of every ancient city. Beggars, cripples, prostitutes, and lepers made up this group. They were the lowest of the low and thus serve to draw the strongest possible contrast to the position of the Rich Man and his kin. They were precisely those who were absent from the concern of the rich, who, believing in the divine construction of the existing order, took pains to isolate themselves from the outcasts with a gulf not unlike that between the Rich Man and Lazarus in Hades. This gulf too was unbridgeable, at least in human terms, given the rigidity of the social stratification in the agrarian city. The status of Lazarus in the story thus highlights the indifference of the upper classes at precisely the points where that indifference was the most socially acceptable in the agrarian world.

We have already noted the significance of Lazarus' name. Such a name, together with the eventual outcome of the story, would have caused true surprise among some of Jesus' listeners who made the usual assumption of late Judaism that the outcast classes were in misery because God was punishing them for their sins. Such a view gives divine justification both to the rich and to their lack of interest in changing the conditions of the poor. The twist given by Jesus to the story thus serves to distinguish what he says from the popular Egyptian and Jewish versions and to sharpen his critique of the rich who use God to justify their position. Here, once again, we meet the familiar use of religion to legitimate the social order, and that, we would contend, is the primary focus of the parable: to warn the rich that they are in for a big surprise.

The use of a figure from the outcast group to draw the contrast with the rich prevents the possibility of a mistaken interpretation that might, had the example been drawn from the lower urban classes who *did* practice the levitical piety, have assumed that Jesus was talking about something less than the eschatological advent of a new age. A poor but pious lower-class person could have been easily imagined resting on the bosom of Abraham by both his peers and the upper classes. The use of such a person in the story might thus have implied the need for mild social reform, but nothing like the coming of a new age. By using the strongest possible sociological contrast, and its total reversal in the end, Jesus highlights the radical, eschatological nature of his warning. He is declaring the imminent appearance of an order in which "what is exalted among men" will become "an abomination in the sight of God" (Luke 16:15). Jesus' warning is not to convince people to believe in life after death, or even a mere prod to compassion for the poor; it is nothing less than the announcement that the eschatological fulfillment of all that was promised in the Scriptures was at hand.

This is how we would take the reference to Moses and the prophets. Jesus is not, as Bultmann suggests, merely asserting the value of the Jewish tradition. He is arguing that the law and the prophets point to what is being fulfilled in the advent of the new age he has announced. That had been the meaning of Jesus' earlier arguments with the elite over the seeking of a sign.[20] They were seeking a sign that the new age had arrived, and Jesus refused to respond for precisely the reasons given in our text: the rich will not heed signs if they will not heed the Scriptures. Our text could thus easily be seen as a commentary on this whole discussion of signs of the new age, a discussion that always takes place in the synoptic Gospels between Jesus and the elite.

Jesus is pointing to a total reversal of values and judgment that will be the mark of the messianic era. He is warning the upper classes of their inability to see it coming because they are looking instead for divine justification of their own position. What they have failed to see in the Scriptures (and would fail to see if the dead were to rise) is that the cry announcing the advent of a new age is the cry of the outcast at the gate. How truly difficult it is for the rich to enter the kingdom of God.

We also cannot help but observe the comments of Max Weber cited earlier that the rich place their hope for honor on their elite sense of identity, while the lower classes rest whatever hope they can muster on the promise of a concealed future.[21] Something very much like that difference of perception is the sociological context of our present text. It is the promise of a new and different future that the figure of Lazarus in the latter half of the story represents, contrasted with the self-justifying attitude the Rich Man maintains to the very end. The surprise ending Jesus gives to the story thus cuts hard across the social perceptions of the agrarian society.

Having said something now of what the text meant in its own agrarian context, our next step is to move into the industrial world of our own day and ask what, if anything, the text means for us. In doing so we shall look first at what the text has been said to mean by preachers and interpreters of our own era, and then comment on the transpositions necessary to bring the text to faithful execution in our day. Since much of our own comment upon this text from a sociological perspective was dependent upon the identity of the two characters in the story, it will be worthwhile by way of comparison to note how the Rich Man and Lazarus are identified by interpreters in the industrial world.

Dr. Hillyer H. Straton, pastor of the First Baptist Church of Malden, Massachusetts, and a widely read author of both books and articles in respected religious journals, has written a book of sermons on the parables of Jesus in which he comments on Luke 16:19–31. These sermons were preached to Straton's Massachusetts congregation in 1959. He describes the Rich Man (Dives) this way:

Although there are references to the Pharisees in the verses immediately preceding, the tone of the parable makes it quite clear that Jesus is here picturing a self-centered Sadducee who does not believe in life after death. . . . "Dives" is not named; he is just any selfish man of wealth.[22]

To William Barclay, the well-known British interpreter who writes popular commentary, "Dives is a figure of indolent self-indulgence, . . . the picture of wealthy luxury."[23] Helmut Thielicke, another well-known preacher from Hamburg, Germany, uses the Rich Man in our text allegorically to symbolize *anyone* who is rich *in whatever sense.*[24] We may not have a lot of money, says Thielicke, but may be

> gifted, intellectually rich people who enjoy good books and interesting characters and look down with contempt upon the "rock and rollers" in our acquaintanceship, the people who go mooching along in the flatland between movies and sex, magazines, comic books, and the stupidities of television.[25]

Thielicke then goes on to explain that there are other ways to be rich as well, such as being rich in love and not having to live life alone. Thielicke then concludes: "In one way or another every one of us has this poor Lazarus lying at our door, since every one, even the poorest of us, is in one way or another a rich man."[26]

Having thus used the Rich Man as an allegorical symbol for each of us today in the varied aspects of our lives, it is appropriate that Thielicke do the same with Lazarus:

> Now, the Bible when it speaks of the "poor" always means a special kind of poverty, which does not necessarily have anything to do with lack of money. It is thinking of publicans and harlots and therefore people who have no merits and no accomplishments to boast of, people who live on the fringe and fag end of life and in this sense are poor. *All of us* at some time in our life have been at this end and thus have been utterly poor and helpless. [Italics mine.][27]

Although not all modern interpreters would allegorize the two characters in the story as thoroughly as Thielicke has done, yet most, including Barclay and Straton, would see them in purely individualistic terms as symbols for any rich or poor person.

To say that we have now moved out of the agrarian world is to put it mildly! All these preachers treat the parable as if it were addressed in highly individualistic terms to the spiritualized and moralistic issues of a rather genteel poverty quite unlike the radical contrast between the Rich Man and Lazarus as we characterized it above. One can perhaps even read in the allegorical interpretation of Helmut Thielicke a search for a context in which to place the story, given the diffusion of meaning that terms like "rich" and "poor" have come to carry in the industrial world. In a sense such an attempt is laudable (and certainly time-honored in the history of preaching!) as an effort at transposition, but it is also so totally individualized that it, like the others cited, misses completely the class connotations of the characters in the text.

This faulty perception of the identity of the two characters in the story has also led the interpreters cited, as well as many others, to equally dubious accounts of the main issue involved in the parable. To Straton, viewing the Rich Man as just any wealthy, self-centered individual, at issue is the moral judgment that "the earthly life of Lazarus would not have been in such a poor state if Dives had been more considerate."[28] To William Barclay the problem is also to be found in the sin of the Rich Man, which in this case is said to be that he didn't "notice" Lazarus.[29] Donald G. Miller, former pastor and seminary president, writing in *The Layman's Bible Commentary*, believes the problem is the materialistic attitudes of people in our society.[30] George Arthur Buttrick, as well-known and respected as any recent American preacher, argues that the point is this:

> It tells us that inequalities on earth are redressed in heaven: lowliness is rewarded hereafter, and self-indulgent pride is rebuked. . . . If a man chooses a cheap heaven here, he can hardly expect to have a real heaven beyond death. . . . The story tells us that life here fashions an eternal destiny.[31]

Like Barclay, Buttrick also believes that the real problem was the sin of Dives in not seeing clearly the needs of Lazarus. To each of these interpreters it is the sins of those isolated individuals for whom the Rich Man is prototypical that constitute the main issue.

This kind of individualistic moralizing about both the Rich Man and Lazarus leads to some assertions that are both tragic and ludicrous at the same time. Says Buttrick: "Wealth is not necessarily wicked, but it has temptations hard to resist; poverty is not necessarily virtue, but it can more easily be turned to the soul's account."[32] What could be a clearer loophole with which to justify both the position of the rich and the misery of the poor! All we have to do to avoid the harsh facts of poverty is to imply their spiritual value: "and every time Lazarus refused to be embittered by the bitter bread of poverty he was building a home in heaven."[33] Here Buttrick is not alone; he is joined by Thielicke, who sees in Lazarus the symbolic occasion for all of us in our moments of spiritual poverty to cast our care upon God.[34] Thus the text is turned into its very opposite: a justification for avoiding the radical injustice of the status quo that our text declares is in the process of being totally reversed by the action of God.

Such examples could be piled up; they are by no means isolated or unique. Not a single one of the preachers cited even mentions the word injustice. Not a single one sets the passage in the eschatological context in which the reversal theme can be taken seriously. Says John Drury, writing in the newer *J. B. Phillips New Testament Commentary:* "Those who do not attend the *smaller things of God*, such as the care for one's neighbor which the Law and Prophets enjoined, are not open to his great works"[35] (italics mine). Smaller works! What could be greater than the advent of the new age? What has happened to the theme of reversal? That God is up to anything serious in the world is totally missing.

Buttrick, picking up the statement of Abraham to the Rich Man in our story ("Son, remember . . ."), writes: "The word is almost 'Child, remember.' Perhaps Dives had never become an adult."[36] He then goes on to point out that those who lack a memory will find that their manhood deteriorates![37]   Still others, such as Miller and Straton, suggest that the remedy for the situation is more charitable use of our riches.   Not only do they not suggest a radical reversal of the social order that creates the injustices of which the parable speaks, they never come close to implying the major point of the story: that *God* is in the process of working out just such a reversal in the eschatological event of the new age, and that the rich are so interested in justifying and solidifying their position that they have missed it altogether.   Is not the charitable use of riches—providing a handout to the poor—exactly what the Rich Man in the story *had been doing*?   His sin, if that were our concern, is more nearly that of charity than the lack of it.   His myopia is such that he allows his very charitableness to prevent him from seeing the deeper questions about a system that creates poverty in the first place, a system of which he is an integral part!   By one means or another, therefore, each of the interpreters cited has taken the radical eschatological orientation of our story and turned it into an exhortation to rich individuals to be nicer to poor people if they care anything about their own personal destiny.   The irony is that this is almost exactly the role played by the Rich Man in the text, whose immediate thought was to warn his rich brothers lest they too fall victim to an evil fate.

What one could or should do with this story in our own day is, once again, the crux of the matter.   It is that which gives us reason to bother with such a text at all.   There are probably many themes embedded in our text that the preacher of today could run with, but these cannot all be detailed here.   What we need to do is point ourselves in the right direction by raising the questions that need to be asked again.   Who are the rich who today justify their position with handouts to the poor, yet never question a system that creates rich and poor?   Where today is the closed corporation of the privileged class which, even when confronted with the radical values of the in-breaking kingdom, thinks nothing of Lazarus or his living relatives but only of how to protect the peer group?   In a society in which the distinctions between rich and poor are exceedingly complex, and in which it is more difficult to draw as sharp a contrast as does the text, how are we to construe the contemporary identity of the two characters in the story? Thielicke sought to do so allegorically, but that turned the text into a moralistic discussion of how we should be, in both the "rich" and "poor" moments of our lives, better people. It is necessary to find transpositions of the text that preserve the radical and eschatological social critique of Jesus' words instead of the typical industrial social perception that religion is addressing the well-being of the individual.

It seems to us that a sermon on this text could preserve the character of Jesus' story and thus faithfully bring the text to execution today, only if the radical sociological contrast and the eschatological warning about its reversal could be preserved. It occurs to us that this could be done in at least two ways. Either the whole thing could be internationalized so as to draw the sharp class distinctions that *do* exist in the wider human family, and thus retain the radical eschatological dimension of the text with a sermon on the human future, or some detailed digging would be required into the poverty issues of present-day America in such a way as to address the text to the *system* and the individual's part in it rather than to the individual alone. Poverty and social class issues do exist in this country, but they must be dealt with in sociologically sophisticated terms that go beyond the simplistic use of terms like "rich" and "poor." Without *something* like this kind of social analysis and critique it would be hard to argue that the text had been faithfully treated in our day.

In summary, it seems to us that with the text we are now considering, just as with that in 1 Kings 21, the sociological perspective is a *necessary* supplement to the usual historical-critical tools in making sure that we have an adequate understanding of the text before we attempt to translate it into our own situation. This same sociological perspective also aids us in identifying the conditions under which the text can properly come to contemporary execution. We share a consanguinity of experience with the agrarian world with respect to the issues of poverty and social injustice, but those issues are more complex and tangled today than in a world that could characterize two people as Jesus did in the story. We also lack consanguinity with the agrarian world in our individualistic temper that goes a long way toward explaining the tendency to moralize the issues rather than treat them eschatologically. We lack the radical sense of world rejection that in the prophetic literature and in the teachings of Jesus produced the sharp ethical dualism of which this text is an example. Even where we do confront issues in our day, we are inclined to see values and ideals as addressing the well-being and maturity of the individual rather than as marks of a coming age.

Finally, we note again that sociological analysis of the pre-understanding which we bring to the text as compared to that of the agrarian society makes clear that the interpretation of a text is not complete until it takes into account the situation of the interpreter. There are *no* uninterpreted places from which interpretation can begin, and that is true not only for the biblical scholar or literary critic but also for the preacher in the present-day pulpit. Our comments about the homiletical contributions of the preachers dealt with above are not meant to cast stones at the efforts of others. They are merely meant to assert that a hermeneutical process which does not take into account both the situation of the interpreter and its relation to that of the text is incomplete. A full hermeneutical method must direct its efforts to every part of the hermeneutical chain, including the critical process by which the preacher turns the text into a contemporary sermon.

6

Highlighting the Interpretive Context

The writer can remember as a small boy hearing a sermon by a well-known preacher on the text of Ephesians 5:15–16: "Look carefully then how you walk, not as unwise men but as wise, making the most of the time, because the days are evil" (RSV). In the industrial society in which time has become a commodity with commercial value, and therefore an item not to be wasted, it was not unnatural to hear this preacher talk to his young audience about the evils of wasting time. We were encouraged to industriousness (!) with the admonition that being Christian and being lazy were mutually contradictory. It all seemed to make great sense or, as the text says, it appeared wise.

In an agrarian society, however, in which time was not a commodity and efficiency not a priority value, the text interpreted in this fashion would not have made sense. Translating from the original, the text properly reads this way: "Take a careful look, therefore, at the way you walk, not as fools but as wise persons. Rescue [*exagorazō*] the opportunity [*kairos*] because the days are evil." Of what opportunity does the Pauline writer speak? And what do the evil days have to do with it? The answers to these questions are much clearer if we remember that the anticipation of the Parousia was still intense at the time Ephesians was written. What else could the opportunity then be than to seize the moment to prepare for the coming of the new age? The opportunity was there to gain the foretaste, the firstfruits of the kingdom. The text is, after all, set in a discussion of maintaining the unity of God's people while standing fast and keeping alert for the coming day. The evil days, the days of the old age yet remaining, are thus a threat to that which is in the process of coming. And since it *is* coming, it would be foolish to lose the opportunity to see and participate in what God is creating.[1]

Ephesians 5:15-16 is thus an encouragement to seize the brief remaining opportunity to taste the firstfruits of the new age and to join with the church as it awaited the coming of the Lord. Since that opportunity would soon be past, it had to be grasped while still available and had nothing to do with the modern industrialized society's notion of time as a commodity not to be wasted. Laying on the text the presuppositions of the industrial world clearly places it in an interpretive context which differs markedly from that in which the text originated.

Throughout our discussion, our primary thesis has been that a part of the conditioning of the interpreter's context—his pre-understanding—is sociological. The questions, perceptions, understandings, and "knowledge" brought to the text ahead of time all influence what we are able to hear the text say, and, in light of that, our contention throughout has been that the conscious investigation of this interpretive context will clarify the conditions under which we can hear today what the text once meant to say.

It is to this end that the preceding exegetical studies have been done. We are suggesting not that such studies produce *the* definitive interpretation—we can never presume that our apprehension of the text is equatable with the text itself—but rather that they provide a step toward clarification of the context in which the interpreter works and therefore aid the translation process. What has been offered in our discussion is thus a paradigm for what obviously could become a very large program of running any and all biblical texts through the sociological grid in order to compare what comes out with the perceptions of interpreters in the industrial world. In the face of such a complex undertaking, it is fortunate that at least some significant human understanding is possible across the barriers of time and culture without waiting for such a program to be completed. But this does not mean that what we are engaged in should be taken lightly. From a negative point of view it offers a serious critique of the overeasy equation between text and interpretation that has perpetually plagued biblical studies. From a more positive point of view such efforts to live at the interface of the two worlds that are trying to communicate with each other promise to deepen mutual understanding. Our studies therefore are meant to highlight the conditioning of the interpretive context in such a way as to clarify the ongoing dialogue between ourselves and the biblical text.

These sociological clarifications to which our exegetical studies have pointed could be used with a great deal of the biblical material, though not all texts involve the rather obvious sociological dynamics evident in the two passages we chose for extended comment. With many texts the sociological conditioning of the interpreter's preunderstanding could easily be overlooked for lack of a clear sociological issue in the text itself. There might be nothing in the text that would trigger a second look on the part of the modern interpreter, and therefore, in the interest of catalyzing a reexamination of a wide variety of biblical material, it will be worthwhile for us to highlight additional texts that illustrate in less obvious ways what it is we have been discussing.

One of the constantly recurring themes of our study so far has been that of the religious legitimation of the social and political order. At this point we today almost certainly share common ground with the agrarian world, though in our society the issue works itself out in somewhat different ways. It ought not, however, to be an issue we have difficulty understanding.

In the agrarian world this legitimation took both political and social forms. It was political insofar as national religions or cultic prescriptions gave divine sanction to the hierarchical sources of power. It was social insofar as it aided the solidification of the social class structure and the privileged position of the rich. In our society the same processes are at work, though in slightly different ways. No particular religion, and certainly not a national religion, provides this kind of cultural legitimation in America. Instead, the divine sanction of our order is invoked by what Robert Bellah has called "civil religion," a faith that is neither Christianity, Judaism, Islam, nor any combination of the three, but rather a fundamental faith that God (or some vaguely defined cosmic reality) is the guarantor of the idealistic vision we have of ourselves and our political structures.[2] The whole matter of religious legitimation is therefore a live one in our society, though care must be exercised in recognizing the differences in the way it functions today as compared to the same process in the agrarian world.

An abundance of biblical texts deal with this issue. A good example is found in Micah 3:9–11: The leaders pronounce judgment for bribes, the priests preach for money, the prophets make divinations for a fee. And yet they rely on Yahweh, saying, "Is not the Lord in the midst of us? No evil shall come upon us." A more graphic indictment of religious legitimation of the social and political order would be hard to find. The juxtaposition in the text of leaders, priests, and prophets pinpoints the issue precisely.

Yet another illustration of the legitimation issue is the controversy over having a king that is described in 1 Samuel 8—12. There the very contemporary issues of military conscription, excessive taxation, arms buildup, and government expropriation of property are all dealt with against a covenant background. These and many other texts like them can surely be used to discuss the legitimation issue today, even though the modern interpreter must take into account the fact that we today do not live in a society that is sociologically stratified the way Israel was, and therefore the effects of religious legitimation are distributed quite differently in our kind of world. Even more to the point is a word of caution about the need to inquire into the relation between the God of civil religion in this country and the God of biblical faith. The complaint of Micah about the leaders, prophets, and priests invoking the presence of Yahweh in hypocritical fashion cannot simply be laid on our society today without taking seriously Robert Bellah's argument that it is not Yahweh who is the object of this country's national "faith" but a vaguely defined cosmic reality that is a personification of the American dream.[3]

Yet another dimension of the problem of religious legitimation is dealt with in a text like Romans 13:1–10. Paul Lehman has pointed out that Paul's comments about obeying civil authorities in that text are usually read as if they stand without qualification, thus requiring of the Christian unreserved obedience to the state. If this were Paul's intent he would appear to be providing a basis for the legitimation of the political status quo, whatever that happened to be. Lehman argues, however, that the paragraphing in most English translations wrenches the text out of its proper context, which would otherwise place strong qualification upon the demand to obey civil authority.[4]

The usual arrangement of this text concludes the paragraph after verse 7, that is, immediately after Paul's comments regarding civil obedience: "Pay all of them their dues, taxes to whom taxes are due, revenue to whom revenue is due, respect to whom respect is due, honor to whom honor is due." The next paragraph then begins: "Owe no one anything, except to love one another; for he who loves his neighbor has fulfilled the law" (v. 8). The implication of this arrangement is that in the new paragraph we have moved to a new subject: the reciprocal, loving relationship with one's neighbor.

Contrary to this usual pattern, Lehman argues that the paragraph break should not divorce Paul's comments about obeying civil authority in verses 1–7 from the more inclusive demand in the following verse to subordinate all other demands to the law of love. Lehman would make verse 8 the concluding, and therefore climactic, statement of the paragraph. It would then read

> . . . For the same reason you also pay taxes, for the authorities are ministers of God, attending to this very thing. Pay all of them their dues, taxes to whom taxes are due, revenue to whom

revenue is due, respect to whom respect is due, honor to whom honor is due. Owe no one anything except to love one another; for he who loves his neighbor has fulfilled the law.

This arrangement implies that obedience to political authorities is ultimately subject to and qualified by the higher demand of love. If such a reading is plausible, Paul is merely restating the old prophetic demand that in the community of God's people all authority is subordinate to the demands of love and justice.

Though there is little that can be claimed either for or against Lehman's reading of this passage from a strictly textual point of view, it at least appears likely that the potential subordination of demands for civil obedience to a higher law of love would more quickly impress readers of the Pauline text who themselves were sociologically sensitive to the issues of hierarchical oppression and injustice. Such a reading would therefore be more likely in a society of rigid social stratification in which hierarchical thinking was normative. This means that a preacher using this text today must deal not only with the fact that the hierarchical mentality has largely disappeared (making the call to obey higher powers culturally and politically awkward) but also with the probability that modern readers will fail to see Paul's juxtaposition of civil obedience with the demand of love. In a society in which the issues of justice are so easily diffused that many people do not recognize them as such (in contrast to the rigid and radical class distinctions of the agrarian world that raised the issues of social justice sharply and invariably), Lehman's point is easily missed.

This latter issue—the ease with which we miss the issue of justice lying beneath so many texts—is graphically illustrated by Paul's dramatic comments concerning the human condition in Romans 1:28–32. Today we are inclined to translate the issues of social justice into those of sin, the *individual's* sin(s), and thus take a text like this one in Romans to be a catalog of the individual human being's problems, on the basis of which Paul then constructs his theology of divine redemption. Yet a simple repunctuation of the text can easily turn it into a radical statement of the conditions of social injustice:

> [28]Since they refused to acknowledge God, God has given them over to their own wicked minds to do what is not proper, steeped in every injustice: [29]perversity, ambition, corruption, puffed up with envy, murder. . . .

The key item is the colon after verse 28. This usage is argued both grammatically and theologically by Jose Miranda, who asserts that the long list of items in verses 29–32 is given by way of qualification of the term "injustice" at the end of verse 28.[5] It is as if Paul believes the fundamental problem of the human condition to be that of social injustice, which can then be defined by the list of qualifiers he gives.

What is of interest to us in this repunctuation of the text is that few persons coming out of an industrial social context would have imagined such a translation. Leaving aside the question of the validity of Miranda's punctuation (though he argues it cogently), it is important to recognize that Jose Miranda, to whom such a translation quite naturally occurs, comes out of a background in an agrarian society.[6] Conditioned as he is by the radical social injustices of the agrarian class system, Miranda sees a word like *adikia* as a red-flag word that he cannot overlook. Cries of injustice, which are basically a critique of the existing *social order* rather than merely of individuals and their private sins, "jump out" of the text for the agrarian mentality in ways that industrially conditioned interpreters simply miss. Miranda thus sees the issue *throughout* Romans to be that of *social* injustice rather than individual sinfulness (though, of course, the two are always linked) and therefore interprets the thrust of Romans as an attack on the religious legitimation of the social order.

The theme of individualism is one that has constantly crept into our discussions so far. We have argued that though the individualism of modern society may have many sources, it is at least partly attributable to (and certainly reinforced by) the economic individualism of the industrial world. We also noted

Bellah's comments that modern religion addresses the well-being of the individual rather than the tension between the world as it is and the social order of prophetic vision. Countless texts could be used to illustrate our tendency today to turn everything into a comment upon individual happiness, maturity, and well-being. We have already seen the propensity for this in Sockman's treatment of 1 Kings 21, and we saw the variety of preachers we looked at in Chapter 5 doing the same thing. To what degree this individualistic mind-set contributes to the excessive moralizing of so much contemporary preaching we do not know, but there is no doubt that many texts interpreted individualistically today would have been read quite differently by the corporate mentality of the agrarian world.

An example of this would be 1 John 4:7–12. There the author talks about our inability to know God unless we love each other. Miranda argues (from the equation of love and justice that he traces from Leviticus 19 through both Old and New Testaments) that love has connotations that move far beyond the one-to-one relationships of individuals. If this is so, then this passage in 1 John, and the many others in the New Testament that speak of loving one's neighbor, should be set in the context of social justice.[7] It is significant that just such an interpretation was given to the parable of the Good Samaritan by Martin Luther King, whereas in the industrial world (at least among those in the middle and upper classes) the usual interpretation of that parable enjoins charity to the needy rather than reform of the system.

A similar example can be found in Paul's discussion of the works of the flesh and the fruits of the Spirit in Galatians 5:13–26. Paul prefaces his comments there with the statement in verse 18, "But if you are led by the Spirit you are not under the law." Paul takes the law to be the normal guarantor of social justice, but since the law has failed in this regard, Paul asserts that this justice should now result from the presence of the Spirit. In this light it is clear that the lists which follow are again lists that address more than the isolated character of the individual. They describe the characteristics of a just and unjust society.

This interpretation is corroborated in Ephesians 4:24. There the Pauline author comments, "Put on the new nature . . . created in the likeness of God in true justice [*dikaiosunē*]"[8] (my trans.). The linking of the "new man" to ideas of social justice is simply not very common among the preachers of the industrial world. It is usually taken merely as a description of the "new being" of the individual, at which point it is appropriate to comment that, Bultmann and others notwithstanding, the notion of "authentic existence" is a decidedly modern one. In spite of Bultmann's arguments that the search for authentic existence is the common denominator in the preunderstanding of both the text and its modern reader, this implies a far more individualistic concept of human existence than can rightly be assumed for the agrarian era.

Perhaps one of the best examples of the individualism with which we today interpret the biblical material is in the typical use of the Beatitudes. These sayings of Jesus are almost invariably taken as a prescription for the well-being of the individual and are isolated both from the issues of social justice and from the eschatological expectation of the new age. It is important to see that many of these Beatitudes exhibit the same reversal-of-fortune theme as did our text in Luke 16:19–31. "Blessed are the ones hungering and thirsting for [justice], for they shall be satisfied" (Matt. 5:6). There the idea of reversal is self-evident and thus justifies setting the saying in an eschatological context. What is not always clear is the relation of the saying to the issues of social justice because of the usual translation of *dikaiosunē*. When translated "righteousness," as it usually is, it conveys the notion of an individualistic quality that it is then assumed will bring personal happiness.[9] But translating *dikaiosunē* with the English term "justice," as would someone from the preindustrial city of an agrarian society,[10] immediately alters one's perception of the entire passage. It now has implications that reach far beyond (though they may include) the well-being of the individual.

This whole problem of the individualistic outlook of modern

industrial societies raises in acute form the larger issue of the sociology of knowledge with which we have been dealing. Given the outlook of the industrial world, *some* accommodation to individualistic thinking is probably a prerequisite for understanding. Individualism is part of our modern preunderstanding and hence the human experience from which we analogize our way to understanding a text. If we were to refuse to use individualistic categories, either from the desire to avoid unwarranted individualistic readings of agrarian texts or because of ideological value judgments placed upon individualism as such, we would sharply limit what the text can say in our day.

It would perhaps be more appropriate to recognize our lack of consanguinity with the social perception of agrarian societies at this point, and then go on to ask what transpositions are possible to make texts reflecting the corporate mentality of the biblical world usable in our society. For example, an attempt could be made to explore the tendency of individualistic thinking to cover up or obscure the issues of social justice (and the individual's implication in them) without passing sweeping negative judgments on other functions of individualism that may have social validity. A sermon using the text in Romans 1:28–32, for example, could *begin* by looking at the individual but not consider the text faithfully treated until the link between the individual's sins and the issues of social justice had been exposed.

Many other biblical texts can be used to illustrate agrarian themes beyond those we have highlighted so far. The extended family that existed among the *upper* classes in the agrarian world, for example, ought perhaps to stimulate a reexamination of genealogies in the Bible, and particularly the genealogies of Jesus. The fact that the latter appear only in Matthew and Luke may be significant if commentators are correct that these two books were written for urban upper classes.[11] It was the upper classes that used genealogies to articulate their sense of continuity and solidarity with their peers. In this light the revolutionary character of the genealogy in Matthew is measurably heightened because its well-known use of five women in the lineage of Jesus must then be seen over against the limited and isolated role of women in the extended families of the upper class.

In the same way, other genealogies in the Bible (which usually hold little interest for the modern reader) may, when seen in a sociological light, reveal issues of identity and continuity as the people of God that have heretofore been overlooked. In our modern world, in which the increasing fragmentation of the family affects nearly every member of society, these genealogies can take on special interest, though it has to be recognized that the sharp upper-class connotations of genealogies in the agrarian world make them inapplicable to our modern society without careful sociological transposition of their implications. They surely have something to say to the contemporary search for roots, if transposed into the context of our industrial world in which roots are less likely to grow from biological soil. Moreover, Luke's extension of the genealogy of Jesus to include the whole human family as such may have value in our day as an inclusive statement that cuts across the lines of class and family fragmentation which have been unwittingly strengthened by the church's tendency to reflect the atomistic social pattern of the industrial world.[12]

A related observation can be made that brings to mind yet another set of biblical texts that have a sociologically conditioned background. We have already cited Lenski's comments about the tendency of different social strata to produce differing accounts of the religious tradition of the community,[13] and observed that this may in part explain the various pentateuchal documents scholars believe can be isolated by means of literary criticism. It is common with those sources to locate them as to date, geography, and historical setting, but far less common is any attempt to do so sociologically. Yet if scholars are correct that the account of creation in Genesis 1, for example, is of priestly composition, and if priests are among the cultural-religious elite of the agrarian society, then it might be possible to view texts such as Genesis 1 as class documents. In that light we could ask the appropriate sociological questions either of this priestly material or of any other sociologically identifiable strata within the Pentateuch (the Gospels?) we wish to interpret. Does Genesis 1 show the typical cultural-religious elitist interest in the routinization and rationalization of the social order, or is this particular text in some radical theological sense atypical of the priestly caste? These and questions like them could appropriately be asked of any New or Old Testament text that can have its source sociologically identified.

Many scholars have pointed to the fact that Christianity first spread among the lower urban classes.[14] In that light it is likely that few New Testament books or particular texts are free of class interest or connotations. Such is the case with Galatians 3:29. Paul, it must be remembered, was both an artisan, who would have shared the outlook of the lower urban classes, and a highly educated intellectual, who would have known the thinking of the elite. He was also a Jew speaking primarily to Gentiles. His call to Christian unity across the barriers of class, race, sex, and nationality is thus made from a unique social and racial position. Its inclusiveness is at one and the same time broader and more sociologically radical than we often suspect. The same is true of many other "unity" texts such as Ephesians 4:1–16 (". . . the whole body, joined and knit together"), Colossians 3:14 (". . . put on love, which binds everything together in perfect harmony"), and many others. It is easy in the industrial society to lose a sense of how radical those statements were in a world split by the yawning gulf between rich and poor, Jew and Gentile.

In our discussion of the perspectives of the various social classes in the agrarian world, we commented upon the propensity of the lower urban classes to emphasize salvation motifs. The upper classes preferred to talk about providence—the preservation of what is. But the lower urban classes (as distinct from the rural peasants or urban outcasts) were more likely to feel what Bellah called "world rejection." That is, they were conscious of the tension between what the world is and what it should be. We say all this not to explain away the New Testament preoccupation with salvation themes but to *explain* it, to make sure we understand it properly by giving it the context it ought to have.

Many commentators have noted the modern tendency to spiritualize the coming of the kingdom of God into an extraterrestrial heaven. The fact is that this is *not* a modern tendency but one that has its roots in the world rejection of agrarian societies. Whereas that world rejection took the form of ethical dualism in ancient Israel, in areas under Persian or Greek influence it came out in the form of a cosmic dualism that rejected the reality and value of the material world. Being the heirs of the Greek tradition, the modern industrialized societies of the West have retained much of this spiritualistic, world-rejecting kind of outlook. Its vestigial remains are intricately interwoven with the newly emerging modern tendency to *accept* the world as a place to experience the multifaceted, largely sensate realities of the world. In our day spiritualism has been bracketed as the domain of religion, in which world rejection remains a dominant motif in a *purely* spiritualistic form. The result of this is that many texts, in spite of scholarly efforts to the contrary,[15] persist in conveying to the modern mind an extraterrestrial vision.[16] One such text, often read at funerals, is Romans 8:18–25. It is worth quoting in full:

I consider that the sufferings of this present time are not worth comparing with the glory that is to be revealed to us. For the creation waits with eager longing for the revealing of the sons of God; for the creation was subjected to futility, not of its own will but by the will of him who subjected it in hope; because the creation itself will be set free from its bondage to decay and obtain the glorious liberty of the children of God. We know that the whole creation has been groaning in travail together until now; and not only the creation, but we ourselves, who have the first fruits of the Spirit, groan inwardly as we wait for adoption as sons, the redemption of our bodies. For in this hope we were saved. Now hope that is seen is not hope. For who hopes for what he sees? But if we hope for what we do not see, we wait for it with patience.

As a text on a salvation motif, this passage in Romans is often interpreted nowadays as portraying the salvation of the individual in an extraterrestrial glorification after death. Gerald R. Cragg, writing in *The Interpreter's Bible,* interprets this text in just this fashion. He discusses it under the rubric, "The Expectation of a Glorified Life."[17] The promise of glory after death is said to be our ultimate destiny in contrast to the suffering of the present existence. Here is clearly a "world-rejection" theme such as Bellah describes, but in this case it is interpreted in a purely individualistic and spiritualistic manner.

Take several of the phrases from Paul's comments in Romans 8, however, and view them both sociologically and eschatologically. If Anders Nygren is right, and we believe he is, that Paul's whole letter to the Romans is set in the context of the two aeons, the old age and the new age,[18] and if the old age can be characterized as the age of injustice (as Paul has done in 1:28–32), then the phrase in verse 18, "the sufferings of the present time," refers not only to the plight of the individual but also to the whole order of social injustice and corruption. The comment in verse 21 that "the creation itself will be set free from its bondage to decay and obtain the glorious liberty of the children of God" becomes a commentary on a new kind of social order of which the children of God are but the firstfruits. No wonder "the creation waits . . . for the revealing of the sons of God" (v. 19) which will signal the arrival of the new era.

The hope of a new age was the characteristic hope of the lower classes, a new age in which there would be a reversal of value and judgment brought in by the presence of the Spirit of God. Without that dream, there was no content to the term "hope." Says Paul, "For in this hope we were saved." Without getting into a discussion of life after death, it can at least be said that salvation motifs such as that in Romans 8 would have had a substantially more historico-eschatological orientation in an agrarian society than they do in our day. That they would also have had a sociologically more radical connotation is indicated by the phrase "the sufferings of the present time." To the interpreter in an industrial context that statement is likely to be seen as describing a sense of personal loneliness or alienation or loss of human meaning. To Paul, as to most lower-class people in the agrarian world, it would have referred to the sufferings of the poor, who felt the radical injustices of the present order and thus looked to God as the source of their hope for a coming new age.

Examples like these we have been citing could be multiplied many times over. The issues of religious legitimation of the social order, of corporate versus individual thinking, of the role and place of the family, of the sociological connotations of terms like "salvation," "righteousness," "suffering," and "hope," and a host of other items could be cited as grist for the preacher's mill in trying to bring the text to faithful execution in our day. Just as scholars have taught us the necessity of living in the historical world of the first century if we are to understand the literature that era produced, so we are suggesting the need to live in the *sociological* world of that same era if we wish to deepen and clarify our understanding still further.

Even more, we are suggesting that by highlighting the industrial society's conditioning of our social perception *in relation to* the sociological context of the biblical text, we can explore and broaden our mutually shared language. The illustrations cited in this chapter are only a small number of what could obviously be a vast set of texts that bear reexamination. It is hoped, therefore, that the highlighting of this kind of analysis might encourage the preacher to place himself in the agrarian world, to compare that world to his own, and then to move to the biblical literature with both greater understanding and renewed appreciation.

HOLBROOK LIBRARY
PACIFIC SCHOOL
OF RELIGION

7

The Preacher as a Link in the Hermeneutical Chain

It has always puzzled a substantial portion of the Christian community to learn that widely divergent interpretations have consistently emerged whenever earnest interpreters studied a given text. No matter what text was used or what historical or geographical location the interpreting was being done in, there has rarely been unanimity on the meaning of Scripture. It would be foolish, of course, to suggest that it will ever be otherwise, but unless the text is to be lost in a hopeless relativism in which each interpreter has a unique and private interpretation, the struggle to expand our capacity for dialogue with the Scriptures must go on. And it must go on not merely in the hope of recovering the literature of antiquity for its own sake but in the expectation that the theological event to which the Scriptures originally bore witness will be re-created in our own day.

In spite of all scholarly efforts to uncover the "true" meaning of biblical texts, diversity of interpretation remains prevalent and problematical. This is the case not because we would somehow be better off if one universal and definitive interpretation could eventually be uncovered, but because the sheer fact of diverse interpretation throws up before us the specter of our subjectivity. It raises the question of whether the Scriptures are speaking *to us* or we are speaking *through them*. While no one would seriously argue that it is possible to understand the Scriptures or anything else except through one's own subjective processes, nonetheless without some effort to give an accounting of, and thus minimize, these subjective factors, we would indeed be left with questions about whether it is the text or ourselves doing the speaking.

All literary interpretation is thus the result of an interplay of subjective and objective factors. Indeed, without both of these items no real understanding could take place. Interpretation, just as authorship, always takes place in an interpretive context in which one brings to the text a *pre*-understanding of the world, of his own situation, of the subject matter with which the text deals, and of what in the text is or is not likely to be relevant to one's own concern. Moreover, life is constantly in the process of creating new contexts in which interpretation can take place and thereby reshuffling the mix of factors that go into the interpretive effort. It is thus not surprising that out of this dynamic and changing situation should come changing interpretations of a given text.

It should also be clear that the context in which the interpreter works furnishes at one and the same time the basis for both understanding and misunderstanding the text. To the degree that the context of the interpreter and the text overlap, there is ground for communication. Without *some* such overlap understanding would be impossible. That such overlap does exist, and that people *can* understand each other across substantial barriers of time and place, is a clear *assumption* on the part of all who make the effort to read the Scriptures, for without it the effort would not be worthwhile. Yet the work we have been doing in the foregoing chapters likewise assumes that the overlap in the context of the text and the interpreter needs substantial enlargement if the dialogue between the two is to be more than superficial. The more the interpreter is able to live at the interface of his own world with that of the text, and to speak the language of both worlds as they are brought together, the greater will be the opportunity for understanding that reaches significant theological depth.

If the overlapping context of text and interpreter furnishes the basis for communication between the two, it is also the disjunctions between these respective contexts that furnishes the basis for misunderstanding. In the terms we have been using, it is where the agrarian and industrial worlds are sufficiently dissimilar that it becomes difficult to carry language across the interface without further considerations. That such areas of disjunctive social perception are substantial should give us pause for thought in any attempt to equate our interpretations with the text itself—or perhaps even more to the point, should make us hesitate before transferring whatever normative quality we assume for the text to our interpretations of it. The preacher who confidently prefaces his theological assertions with the formula "The Bible says" is only an obvious illustration of the tendency to equate text and interpretation that has plagued biblical studies from the start. The ever-new contexts that emerge in the flow of human life are constantly adding opportunities for both new understanding and new misunderstanding, and will continue to do so as long as social change is with us. Thus we can assert that reexamining biblical texts in the manner we have been doing presumes on the one hand that we cannot absolutize (or universalize) our interpretations, and on the other that we are not lost in such utter subjectivity that meanings cannot be shared across the barriers of time and place. People from diverse contexts can understand each other, but they can do so with greater clarity and depth when they make the effort to live in each other's world.

In the course of our discussion each element in the hermeneutical chain that stretches from text to interpreter has been of concern to us. There is first of all the text itself and what it meant originally to say. The historical-critical studies of the last century have done much to illumine the historical context in which the biblical literature was produced. To whatever degree this has been successful, a measure of objectivity has been introduced into the interplay of factors that affect interpretation. Moreover, the highlighting of this historical data has in turn accentuated the datedness of the biblical writings themselves. At the same time that such studies sought to bridge the gap of years and place, they have ironically made the existence of that gap so much the clearer.

Our argument has been, however, that valuable though these historical studies have been, they are not enough to account for what the text once meant to say. Sociological factors must also be taken into account. It is not enough to know that the Gospel of Matthew was written just after the fall of Jerusalem from somewhere in Syria-Palestine. Nor is it enough to know that it may have been written by a Jewish Christian for Jewish Christians. We also need to know if it was written by and for the upper classes. We need to know the sociological context of the characters, the events, the language, and even the form of Matthew's stories. Without this kind of information our ability to understand what the text once meant to say is limited significantly. No doubt disciplines other than historiography and sociology could add still further to the explication of the context of the text, but at present we are simply concerned to make the case for sociological investigation as critical to understanding the context in which the text was written and first understood.

The second element in our discussion has been the sociological explication of the context of the interpreter. We have argued that it too is a key item in the interplay of factors that are at work in the hermeneutical process. If hermeneutics is to be more than merely saying what the text *once* meant, and includes a concern for the conditions under which the text may say something to us *today*, then the context of the interpreter himself must be taken into account.

The urgent need to look at the context of the interpreter seems clear for several reasons. Not only is there the matter of concern for whatever biases the interpreter's context may introduce into his work, but there is also the fact that those biases will exercise their effect most virulently precisely when they remain the most unconscious. Even when raised to consciousness the perceptions that influence the modern mind do not cease to function, but when left below the level of conscious thought they almost certainly influence our interpretation more than we have cared to admit.

Yet another concern about the interpreter's context arises from the notion common in the school of thought that speaks of its work as the "new hermeneutic."[1] The concern of these theologians has been for the *functionality* of words.[2] That is, words sometimes do more than pass along information that can be designated true or false. Sometimes words *do* something rather than *describe* something—as in a declaration of war or the taking of a wedding vow. An *event* occurs by virtue of the words being said. Such words may not be verifiable as true or false in the positivistic sense, but neither are they nonsense. They actually bring events into being and hence have a *performative* function. It is in this sense that these scholars speak of the Scriptures as a "language event," that is, as a word that means to perform a function or carry out an act.

The "event" of Scripture can take a variety of forms. Sometimes it comes to us in the form of promise, and like a wedding vow the promise means to bring into being that which is promised. At other times the "event" created by the words is a call to decision, a demand, such as is the intent of many of Jesus' parables. The words are intended to have an effect, and when they do they can be said to have become a "word event."

Gerhard Ebeling, Ernst Fuchs, and other proponents of the new hermeneutic thus assume that the intention of any text today is to reproduce the same word event as was brought into being at the time of the text's original hearing. At least part of what gives the Scriptures their normative significance for the church today is their ability to be heard in such a way that these language events reoccur. Moreover, it is the use of the text in a way that allows these recurring events to happen that is a primary function of preaching. In a sense, then, the intention of the text is *not* executed in a mere descriptive account of what the text once said. The words are only given faithful reexpression when the promise is again made, the demand for decision again heard, or the liberation of the oppressed again accomplished with rejoicing. All of which means, of course, that the conditions under which the interpreter approaches the text will not only color what he hears the text to have once said, but will also enhance or block the functionality of the word that seeks expression in our own day.

This concern for the functionality of the word is the level of interpretation that most directly concerns the preacher. It is ultimately his interpretive context and that of the people who hear him speak which is the arena wherein a new language event must take place. Without presuming theologically to limit or proscribe the self-revelation of God (or to deny that God's word has been heard in all kinds of contexts, however well or poorly understood), still the character and makeup of the particular context of a particular preacher or listener is clearly a major factor in setting the limits for what can and cannot be heard from the text. Indeed, this is yet another aspect of that scandal of particularity that is written across virtually every page of the Scripture itself.

When this problem of the interpretive context that we have been discussing is pushed one step further, into the situation of a congregation listening to the preached word, the complexity of the factors affecting interpretation threatens to become overwhelming. This is a problem with which every preacher is well acquainted. No two people sitting in a congregation share precisely the same social perception of reality, nor do they bring to the hearing of the text the same preunderstanding with which to hear it. Not only are preachers familiar with this, but also most of them have been amazed at some of the things people have "heard" them say. The logic of this, if pushed too far, would bring us once again to a hopeless relativism in which the text means something different to each person it addresses. Though there may be a sense in which this is true, nonetheless it is also a fact that people do understand each other. And they do, because for all the particularity of their individual perception of the world, people also share perceptions and common experiences such that communication does occur. Without consanguinity of perception and experience, congregations would not form. People would be reduced to silence in the presence of each other. Highlighting this *common* preunderstanding, therefore, allows us not only to assess how it may be coloring our reading of Scripture but also to focus and clarify the basis we share for understanding each other in our own society. That is, *it clarifies the conditions under which the text can come to execution in our own day.* And that, we would contend, in addition to the matter of ascertaining what the text once said, is a major role of the interpreter in our day.

This task of clarifying the conditions under which the text can come to execution today is, it seems to us, especially incumbent upon the preacher. He, being a major link in the hermeneutical chain, cannot presume to take a supposedly universal interpretation of a biblical text that has been uncovered by scholars and preach that in his own situation without first asking what effect it will produce and if that effect is the same one the text originally intended to produce. He must ask himself what the text will *perform* if preached in this way in his situation. That is the key question, and that is what creates the necessity of raising to consciousness the perceptions and preunderstanding of a particular parish or particular preacher in the process of turning the text into a sermon.

Our thesis in the present inquiry has been that the highlighting of the *sociology* of the preacher (and congregation) is an essential item in this process of clarifying the conditions under which the text is heard. In the same way that it was important to know if Luke 16:19–31 was or was not written to the upper classes, so also it is important to know if it is or is not being preached to the upper classes. If it is, one must then ask if the conditions under which they are hearing it will allow for confrontation with the same call to decision that was created by the text originally. If not, that is, if the text is being addressed today to someone other than the upper classes, then what of its original function can the text perform? What is likely in many congregations in an industrial society is that the text is being addressed to an audience made up of many classes and of persons who participate simultaneously in several classes. How then is the text to be faithfully used? Whatever conclusions a given preacher may reach on these issues, it seems clear that a diminished opportunity even to ask these questions exists without some understanding of the sociology of what is going on. It could even be argued that a conscious knowledge of the sociological aspects of the interpretive context of both text and preacher would in and of itself be a small step toward using the text appropriately.

The final concern of our inquiry that must be summarized and highlighted is the *relationship between* the two poles of the hermeneutical process we have just been discussing, that is, the respective contexts of text and interpreter. Here we have asked the questions not just about the sociological setting of each pole in the relationship but about the sociology *of their knowledge*. That is to say, we have inquired about the social perception of reality (and hence preunderstanding) which the text and the interpreter may or may not share. Put another way, we must not only know if Luke 16:19–31 was addressed to the upper classes, and if it is being addressed to the upper classes in our day, but also *how upper-class people then and upper-class people now perceive the world*.

We have asked about consanguinity of experience and perception as well as the lack thereof. We have noted the common experience of using religion to legitimate the social order, but have also seen that among different social groups in the same society, and among the same social groups in different societies, this legitimation does not work the same way. We have seen that the agrarian world, with its stark and rigid class distinctions, addressed its faith to the issues of social justice and the corporate well-being of the human family. The industrial society, on the other hand, characterized by greater class mobility and diffusion, has addressed its religious concern to the well-being of the individual. Thus a phrase like "the righteousness of God" does not mean the same thing in both societies. To the agrarian society it had to do with the justice to which God calls humanity. In an industrial society it is more likely to mean the moral quality of life to which God calls the individual.

We have thus argued that the *starting point* of the interpreter is itself conditioned, sociologically as well as historically. There can be no universal interpretations because there is no universal perception of reality. But there can be understanding in large measure because not *all* human experience is disjunctive and not *all* human perception is unique. Meanings can be shared. And they can increasingly be shared as we learn to live in and understand the social perceptions of each other's worlds. The dialogue between text and interpreter is thus broadened and deepened by the attempt of the modern interpreter to immerse himself in the social perceptions of the biblical world and to draw the correlations between those and his own.

There are those today, of course, who would argue that all this analysis is not necessary. They point to what they call "simple faith" among unsophisticated readers of Scripture and argue that understanding of the biblical literature can take place without all the complex analysis in which we have been involved. In one sense they are right. Not *all* human experience is unique, and therefore points of consanguinity between ourselves and the biblical writers do exist that give us a basis for reading the text without the complexities of scholarship. Yet in another sense we today are the victims of a complex situation that only the obscurantist can overlook. If the ground of common understanding between ourselves and the text is to be more than superficial, a tremendous amount of work is necessary in uncovering the biases of our perception. We must make the effort to expand the consanguinity of experience between ourselves and the text that will enable us to comprehend with greater depth and to limit our claims for shifting the authority of the text to our interpretations of it.

In a way it is incredibly ironic that people in the world today who are still living in agrarian societies and thus lack many of the benefits of modern education often read the Bible with more ease and insight than those of us who possess the intellectual sophistication and educational skills of the industrial society.[3] To a degree this can be seen in the work of Jose Miranda. Although he is a highly educated and skilled exegete, yet his roots in the agrarian society make evident to him things that can only be seen in the text by an interpreter from an industrialized society after exhaustive critical analysis. Living in the complex world of today, we have become victims of the distance we have put between ourselves and the agrarian world out of which the Bible came. We thus have no choice but to use analytical skills to draw the correlations between our world and the one we have irrevocably left behind. As someone has said, in the industrial society true simplicity lies on the far side of complexity, and on the near side lies simplemindedness! Those who share the social perception of reality of the agrarian society by virtue of still living in that world today may indeed share a larger reservoir of common language with the Bible than do the rest of us. But for those of us who do not, the acquisition of that common language comes only after a substantial commitment to live with and differentiate the complex interface between the two worlds.

Recognizing the sociologically conditioned status of our knowledge about the world places special burdens upon the preacher. He cannot be content to call biblical scholarship a descriptive science that has completed its task when it has spelled out what the text once meant. His primary concern is that the word become a *new* event in the act of preaching, and therefore clarity about the conditions under which that can happen is the special need of anyone who attempts to produce the transition from text to sermon. It is the preacher's task to concentrate not only on the ancient (textual) half of the bipolar conversation, nor only on the modern end either, but precisely on the conditions under which the one becomes the other. Preaching is not merely the presentation of an agreed-upon interpretation of a given text. If that were so, the interpretations of the scholars could simply be repeated universally without regard to the time or place of the audience. But if we have been right in arguing that this cannot be done and still bring the text to *faithful* execution, then it becomes the special joy and agony of the preacher to keep text and contemporary interpretation together and to know how the one becomes the other. Put another way, not only must he ask what the text meant in an agrarian society, and thus what it means to say to us, but he must also know how in the peculiar interpretive context of his own world it is possible to make the text say the same thing.

One final observation seems warranted from the brief discussion we have been conducting. What has been done in our investigations of 1 Kings 21 and Luke 16, and has been hinted at with a number of other passages, could obviously become an entire program of hermeneutical inquiry. Few commentaries in print today take either sociology or the sociology of knowledge into account, and those that do are just a small beginning. No doubt in the next few years a great deal will be done in looking at the Scriptures in these ways, just as in the past a massive effort was made to do so historically. But between these two efforts there exists one significant difference that will change the situation. It was possible for the preacher to allow the historical scholar to go about his work in a detached and objective manner, appropriating the results of that work as needed. But the program we are suggesting now cannot be done that way because the particular preacher in a particular sociological context is *himself* a part of the hermeneutical formula we have been developing. It is not some scholar's context that will determine the conditions under which the text can become a sermon, but that of the preacher himself. And thus without direct involvement on the part of the preacher, who takes responsibility for his own interpretive context and what that is doing to the execution of the text, the entire hermeneutical process will be aborted immediately before it comes to fruition.

The preacher is increasingly and inescapably a part of the hermeneutical chain. With the pace of social change being what it is today, it will be increasingly difficult to lay down universal categories that, when applied to the text, will automatically issue in a faithful interpretation. To put the matter simply and directly, as biblical scholarship increasingly raises to the conscious level a hermeneutical process that includes the text, the interpreter, the relation between the two, and the conditions under which the text becomes a sermon, the ball is moving closer and closer to the preacher's side of the hermeneutical court.

Notes

Chapter 1

1. James M. Robinson, "The Future of New Testament Theology," *Religious Studies Review* 2, no. 1 (January 1976): 17.

2. Gerhard Ebeling, "Word of God and Hermeneutic," in *New Frontiers in Theology* (New York: Harper & Row, 1964), 2:93.

3. Ibid., pp. 93 ff.

4. Ibid., p. 109.

5. Rudolf Bultmann, "The Problem of Hermeneutics," in *Essays*, trans. James C. G. Grieg (London: SCM Press, 1955), pp. 257 ff.

6. Ibid., p. 256.

7. This point has been made well by Robert W. Funk, "The Hermeneutical Problem and Historical Criticism," in *New Frontiers in Theology*, 2:165.

8. Ernst Fuchs, *Studies of the Historical Jesus*, trans. A. Scobie (London: SCM Press, 1964), pp. 206, 212; Gerhard Ebeling, "Word of God and Hermeneutic," pp. 93–96, 109.

9. Robert W. Funk, *Language, Hermeneutic and the Word of God* (New York: Harper & Row, 1966), p. 11.

10. Bultmann, "The Problem of Hermeneutics," p. 238.

11. Dorothee Soelle, *Political Theology*, trans. John Shelley (Philadelphia: Fortress Press, 1974), p. 56.

Chapter 2

1. Dan Otto Via, Jr., *The Parables: Their Literary and Existen-*

tial Dimension (Philadelphia: Fortress Press, 1967), p. 40.

2. Wilhelm Dilthey, *Patterns and Meaning in History* (New York: Harper & Row, 1962), pp. 67–68.

3. Peter L. Berger and Thomas Luckmann, *The Social Construction of Reality* (Garden City, N.Y.: Doubleday & Co., 1966), p. 24.

4. Ibid., p. 28.

5. Ibid., p. 25.

6. Ibid., p. 24.

7. Ibid.

8. Peter L. Berger and Thomas Luckmann, "Sociology of Religion and Sociology of Knowledge," in *Sociology of Religion*, ed. Roland Robertson (New York: Penguin Books, 1969), p. 66.

9. Wilhelm Dilthey, to whom this notion can probably be traced, has rightly been criticized for seeing this preunderstanding as too inward and subjective. Cf. James M. Robinson, "Hermeneutic Since Barth," in *New Frontiers in Theology* (New York: Harper & Row, 1964), 2:69–70.

10. Rudolf Bultmann, "The Problem of Hermeneutics," in *Essays*, trans. James C. G. Grieg (London: SCM Press, 1955), pp. 239–43.

11. Robert W. Funk, "The Hermeneutical Problem and Historical Criticism," in *New Frontiers in Theology*, 2:189.

12. Berger and Luckmann, *The Social Construction of Reality*, p. 7.

Chapter 3

1. Gerhard E. Lenski, *Power and Privilege* (New York: McGraw-Hill, 1966), p. 190.

2. Gideon Sjoberg, *The Pre-Industrial City* (New York: The Free Press, 1960), p. 13.

3. Ibid., p. 10.

4. Sociologists in the field of macrosociology are not even in agreement on the appropriate terminology for these societies. Sjoberg prefers the term "feudal" for what Lenski calls the

"agrarian" society. Robert Bellah refers to this same social structure as "historic society." We have chosen to adopt Lenski's terminology in the main, though when dealing with the development of religious thought in a historical perspective we will have occasion to use and describe Bellah's terms as well.

5. The following description of the characteristics of agrarian society is taken largely from Lenski, *Power and Privilege,* pp. 190–297.

6. It is this fact that has led Bellah to adopt the term "historic" society to describe what we are calling agrarian. We note this carefully since we intend to use Bellah's distinctions below.

7. As a parenthetical note, one cannot help but call attention to this fact in light of Albrecht Alt's now classic reconstruction of the formation of Israel as a peaceful infiltration of nomads into the uninhabited areas of Canaan. The sociological bias of Alt's preunderstanding as he interpreted the texts in Joshua and Judges is surely here called into question.

8. The city as it existed in the agrarian world is what Sjoberg has called the "pre-industrial" city. To clarify his terminology he introduces two synonyms: the "pre-industrial civilized society" and the "literate pre-industrial society." See Sjoberg, *The Pre-Industrial City,* p. 10.

9. It is *very* important here not to be misled by an overeasy use of the term "vocational specialization." The term is a relative one and is not meant to indicate that anything like our present-day specialization and vocational mobility existed in the agrarian world.

10. Lenski, *Power and Privilege,* p. 209.

11. It is worth noting here Herman Waetjen's thesis that the Gospel According to Matthew originated in an urban context, while the Gospel According to Mark has a setting in the rural countryside. See Herman Waetjen, *The Origin and Destiny of Humanness* (Corte Madera, Calif.: Omega Books, 1976), p. 28.

12. Sjoberg, *The Pre-Industrial City,* p. 109. Note also how Sjoberg defines social class: "For us, a social class is a large body

of persons who occupy a position in a social hierarchy by reason of their manifesting similarly valued objective criteria."

13. For what follows we are primarily indebted to: Sjoberg, *The Pre-Industrial City*, pp. 108–320; and Max Weber, *The Sociology of Religion*, trans. Ephraim Fischoff (Boston: Beacon Press, 1963), pp. 46–137 and 223–61.

14. Lenski, *Power and Privilege*, p. 214.

15. Ibid., p. 218.

16. Sjoberg, *The Pre-Industrial City*, p. 132.

17. Ibid., p. 161.

18. Ibid., p. 159.

19. Weber, *The Sociology of Religion*, p. 85.

20. Ibid., pp. 85–89.

21. Ibid., pp. 90 ff.

22. Ibid., p. 107.

23. Ibid., p. 98.

24. Ibid., pp. 84–85, 96.

25. Ibid., p. 81.

26. Max Weber, *Ancient Judaism* (Glencoe, Ill.: The Free Press, 1952), p. 387.

27. See, for example, Rabbi Hillel (30 B.C.–A.D. 20), *Aboth* 2.6. He states, "No brutish man is Godfearing; nor is one of the people of the land [*am ha aretz*] pious."

28. *Mishna Hagiga* 3.4.

29. Weber, *The Sociology of Religion*, p. 106.

30. Lenski, *Power and Privilege*, p. 297.

31. This profile is taken primarily from ibid., pp. 297–433.

32. Ivan Illich, *Deschooling Society* (New York: Harper & Row, 1971).

33. Lenski, *Power and Privilege*, pp. 308 ff.

34. Sjoberg, *The Pre-Industrial City*, pp. 163 ff.; Lenski, *Power and Privilege*, pp. 402–6.

35. Sjoberg, *The Pre-Industrial City*, p. 140.

36. Robert Bellah, "Religious Evolution," in *Sociology and Re-*

ligion, ed. Norman Birenbaum and Gertrude Lenzer (Englewood Cliffs, N.J.: Prentice-Hall, 1969), pp. 67–83.

37. Ibid., p. 68.

38. Bellah does not deny that there are profound differences among these various rejections of the world and their consequences for human action. Theologians would doubtless insist that such differences are decisive. Nonetheless, idealism in any form implies a disjunction between what is and what ought to be and hence involves at least some negative judgment about the world and/or the human enterprise. See also Max Weber, "Religious Rejections of the World and Their Directions," in *From Max Weber,* ed. Hans H. Gerth and C. Wright Mills (New York: Oxford University Press, 1946).

39. Bellah, "Religious Evolution," pp. 74–75.

Chapter 4

1. Dan Otto Via, Jr., *The Parables* (Philadelphia: Fortress Press, 1967), p. 22.

2. This point has been made by Walter Wink, *The Bible in Human Transformation* (Philadelphia: Fortress Press, 1973), pp. 1–18.

3. Via, *The Parables,* p. 23.

4. The distinction between what the text *meant* and what it *means* is one drawn by Krister Stendahl.

5. 1 Kings 16:30.

6. Cf. Josephus *Antiquities* 8.13.8: "Ahab was glad at what had been done, and rose up immediately from the bed whereupon he lay."

7. Norman Snaith, in *The Interpreter's Bible,* vol. 3 (Nashville: Abingdon Press, 1954), pp. 176–77.

8. 1 Kings 16:31.

9. See Deut. 17:6.

10. John Gray, *I and II Kings: A Commentary* (Philadelphia: Westminster Press, 1970), p. 438.

11. Snaith, in *The Interpreter's Bible*, p. 174; Gray, *I and II Kings*, p. 440.

12. The usual interpretation, of course, is that Naboth is a poor and humble peasant!

13. For a detailed and interesting discussion of the socio-juridical background of 1 Kings 21, see Francis I. Andersen, "The Socio-Juridical Background of the Naboth Incident," *Journal of Biblical Literature* 85 (1966): 46–57.

14. Ralph W. Sockman, *The Interpreter's Bible*, 3:177 ff.

15. Ibid., p. 178.

16. Ibid.

17. Ibid., p. 179.

18. See our discussion of this in Chapter 3.

19. See our criticism of Bultmann at exactly this point in Chapter 2.

Chapter 5

1. Rudolf Bultmann, *History of the Synoptic Tradition*, trans. John Marsh (New York: Harper & Row, 1963), p. 178.

2. Hugo Gressmann, cited by Joachim Jeremias, *The Parables of Jesus*, rev. ed. (London: SCM Press, 1963), p. 183.

3. Jeremias, *The Parables of Jesus*, p. 183.

4. Ibid.

5. Frank W. Beare, *The Earliest Records of Jesus* (Nashville: Abingdon Press, 1963), p. 182.

6. Notably Bultmann and Beare.

7. Bultmann, *History of the Synoptic Tradition*, pp. 178, 196, 203 ff.

8. The same point is made by the Egyptian version of the story.

9. See John D. Crossan, *In Parables* (New York: Harper & Row, 1973), pp. 66 ff.

10. The allusion in the story to resurrection may in fact be the result of redaction by the early church in an attempt to use the text as a polemic against the Jews for their refusal to be-

lieve in spite of the resurrection of Jesus. In its *present* form the story may reflect the needs of the church. But the *main point* of the story, as we shall argue shortly, is not resurrection or life after death or a polemic against the Jews as such, but the advent of an eschatological reality in which there is to be a total reversal of value and judgment.

11. Luke 1:51–53; Luke 6:20 ff.

12. Jeremias, *The Parables of Jesus*, pp. 37 ff.

13. J. M. Creed, *The Gospel According to St. Luke* (London: Macmillan & Co., 1930), p. 209; Jeremias, *The Parables of Jesus*, p. 186.

14. Once again the attribution of the main thrust of the parable to Jesus and his situation does not prevent seeing the matter of resurrection as relating to the needs and situation of the church.

15. Jeremias, *The Parables of Jesus*, p. 184.

16. Ibid., p. 185.

17. Creed, *The Gospel According to St. Luke*, p. 214.

18. Crossan, *In Parables*, pp. 66–67.

19. Jeremias, *The Parables of Jesus*, p. 186.

20. Matt. 12:38–39; Matt. 16:1–4; Mark 8:11–13; Luke 11:29.

21. Max Weber, *The Sociology of Religion*, trans. Ephraim Fischoff (Boston: Beacon Press, 1963), p. 106.

22. Hillyer H. Straton, *A Guide to the Parables of Jesus* (Grand Rapids: Wm. B. Eerdmans Pub. Co., 1959), p. 188.

23. William Barclay, *The Gospel of Luke* (Philadelphia: Westminster Press, 1956), p. 222.

24. Helmut Thielicke and William Barclay are not Americans and might initially be judged to introduce a new dimension to our discussions, yet it can be argued that living as they do in highly industrialized societies they share many of the same social perceptions as those of us on the western side of the Atlantic.

25. Helmut Thielicke, "The Parable of the Rich Man and Lazarus," in *Great Expository Sermons*, ed. F. D. Whitesell (Westwood, N.J.: Fleming H. Revell Co., 1964), p. 182.

26. Ibid., p. 183.

27. Ibid., p. 185.

28. Straton, *A Guide to the Parables of Jesus,* p. 190.

29. Barclay, *The Gospel of Luke,* p. 222.

30. Donald G. Miller, "The Gospel According to Luke," in *The Layman's Bible Commentary,* ed. Balmer H. Kelley (Richmond: John Knox Press, 1959), pp. 123–24.

31. George Arthur Buttrick, "Exposition (Chs. 13–18)," *The Interpreter's Bible,* vol. 8 (Nashville: Abingdon Press, 1952), p. 290.

32. Ibid., p. 289.

33. Ibid., p. 290.

34. Thielicke, "The Parable of the Rich Man and Lazarus," p. 186.

35. John Drury, "Luke," *The J. B. Phillips New Testament Commentary* (New York: Macmillan Co., 1973), p. 162.

36. Buttrick, "Exposition," p. 291.

37. Ibid., p. 292.

Chapter 6

1. The apocalyptic character of the text we are here citing raises in general terms the issue of the relation of apocalyptic thought to the world of the agrarian society. Two matters discussed earlier will help us clarify this relationship.

We noted Robert Bellah's comments about the rise of an outlook of "world rejection" that corresponded historically with the appearance of agrarian societies. Bellah gives no account of any cause-and-effect relationship but simply observes that these two phenomena appear simultaneously. In Judaism this world rejection, which is a key feature of apocalyptic thought and which in early Israel was primarily an ethical dualism, increasingly took on the cosmic connotations characteristic of Persian thought. Most interpreters argue that this cosmic dualism penetrated Jewish thought in the exilic and postexilic periods and was mediated by Judaism to early Christianity.

We have also cited Max Weber's comments that dissatisfaction with the state of things, and thus a felt tension between the way things were and the way they should have been, was characteristic of the lower urban classes of agrarian societies. It was they, unlike the upper classes who valued a sense of their own being, who looked for a promised new order in the future. The implication of Weber's comments is that it was the appearance of the striking and rigid differentiations of social class that accompanied the rise of agrarian societies which was responsible for this dissatisfaction and the consequent eschatological expectation. In the earlier horticultural (Bellah's archaic) societies such disparity of social class did not exist, and thus religious thought tended to be an articulation of the dance of cosmic harmony.

It would be foolish, of course, to argue that the origins of apocalyptic thought are completely attributable to the historic rise of social class distinctions, but for the purposes of our study this partial clarification needs to be made. In addition to these sociological comments, any full accounting of the origins of apocalyptic thought in the New Testament would have considered at length the influence of the eschatological aspects of prophetic thought and the religious dynamics of the New Testament period.

2. The original article by Robert Bellah on "civil religion" is in William G. McLoughlin and Robert N. Bellah, *Religion in America* (Boston: Houghton Mifflin, 1968), pp. 3–23. See also Robert N. Bellah, *Beyond Belief: Essays on Religion in a Post-Traditional World* (New York: Harper & Row, 1970), pp. 168–92.

3. Ibid., pp. 168–72.

4. Discussed in a lecture at San Francisco Theological Seminary, July 1976.

5. Jose P. Miranda, *Marx and the Bible: A Critique of the Philosophy of Oppression* (Maryknoll, N.Y.: Orbis Books, 1974), pp. 161 ff.

6. It should be noted here that Miranda is himself from Mexico and moves within the agrarian spirit that still pervades

that country to a much greater degree than is evident in the United States. We ought also to comment that to write Miranda off as a Marxist ideologue can easily become just another upper-class statement of contempt for the passionate religion of the lower classes. In spite of Miranda's passion and occasional excesses, a fair reading of his work reveals that his most basic assumptions are Christian rather than being Marxist in any ideological sense. Nor does Miranda see himself as totally outside the social and cultural system he criticizes. He has addressed his critique to himself as well as to Western society. See ibid., p. xi.

7. Ibid., p. 63. See also the extensive discussion of the equation of love and justice in Joseph Fletcher, *Situation Ethics* (Philadelphia: Westminster Press, 1966), pp. 87–102.

8. For the translation of *dikaiosunē* as "justice," see Miranda, *Marx and the Bible*, pp. 15, 94, 111–12, 175.

9. See the treatment of the Beatitudes in William Barclay, *The Gospel of Matthew* (Philadelphia: Westminster Press, 1956), pp. 78 ff.

10. Miranda, *Marx and the Bible*, p. 226.

11. Many commentators have described this as the audience of Luke. For similar comments on Matthew see Herman Waetjen, *The Origin and Destiny of Humanness* (Corte Madera, Calif.: Omega Books, 1976), pp. 28 ff.

12. See H. Richard Niebuhr, *The Social Sources of Denominationalism* (New York: Holt and Co., 1929).

13. Chapter 3, p. 33.

14. Max Weber, *The Sociology of Religion*, trans. Ephraim Fischoff (Boston: Beacon Press, 1963), pp. 84–85.

15. See, for example, Anders Nygren, *Commentary on Romans* (Philadelphia: Muhlenberg Press, 1949), pp. 16–26, 329–46.

16. We are not denying spiritual reality, only a view of reality that sees the spiritual as the *only* reality with ultimate significance.

17. Gerald R. Cragg, "Exposition of Romans," *The Interpre-*

ter's Bible, vol. 9 (Nashville: Abingdon Press, 1954), p. 518.

18. Nygren, *Commentary on Romans,* pp. 16–26.

Chapter 7

1. The names usually associated with this school of thought are those of Ernst Fuchs and Gerhard Ebeling in Europe, and James Robinson and Robert Funk in this country.

2. Fredrick Ferre, *Language, Logic, and God* (New York: Harper & Row, 1961), pp. 55–56.

3. In conversations with persons working in World Council of Churches agriculture programs in Haiti, the writer has discussed this phenomenon at length. In that country, especially among illiterate peasants, certain bibical concepts are understood with remarkable facility that in this country would require considerable exegesis and translation to make clear.